HAMLET

THE
Tragicall Historie of
HAMLET,

Prince of Denmarke.

By William Shakespeare.

Newly imprinted and enlarged to almost as much againe as it was, according to the true and perfect Coppie.

AT LONDON,
Printed by I. R. for N. L. and are to be sold at his shoppe vnder Saint Dunstons Church in Fleetstreet. 1604.

The Title-page of the "Second Quarto."

SHAKESPEARE'S

HAMLET

PRINCE OF DENMARK

Edited by
JOHN HAMPDEN, M.A.

THOMAS NELSON & SONS LTD
LONDON AND EDINBURGH

First published in this Series April 1930
Reprinted 1934, 1935, 1936, 1937, 1938 (twice)
1939, 1941, 1942

PREFACE

THIS series is planned with one simple aim in view—
to make the reading of Shakespeare's plays as easy
and straightforward as possible.

Notes are reduced to the smallest compass. First,
in order that the reader's imagination may have
definite material to work with, the list of the *dramatis
personæ* is preceded by a suggestion of their dress and
appearance ; and when practicable, illustrations are
given. Second, the text, which is presented without
any further preliminary, is accompanied by footnotes
which form a Glossary of obsolete or misleading words.

The play may therefore be read at first sight without let or hindrance—without even the delay and
distraction which would be caused by turning to a
later page for such merely necessary explanations. But
there will be many for whom, if not at a first reading
yet perhaps at a second, something further may be
desirable—a bit of historical information, a para-
phrase of a difficult passage, or the clearing up of a
confused metaphor. To supply these, and to supply
them at the right time, is the object of the brief notes
placed immediately after the text.

Fourth, and last, comes a causerie in several divisions : offering, for any who are studiously inclined,
a short commentary ; marking the place of this
particular drama in Shakespeare's career ; tracing its
importance in his poetic development ; estimating
its artistic value ; and suggesting a number of other
questions on which an intelligent student might reflect
with pleasure.

CONTENTS

INTRODUCTION. 8

THE TRAGEDY OF HAMLET 11

ADDITIONAL NOTES 147

HELPS TO FURTHER STUDY:

    I. The Text of Shakespeare's Plays . 161

    II. The Text and Date of *Hamlet* . . 167

    III. The Source of the Play . . . 172

    IV. The Revenge Plays and *Hamlet* . . 173

ON THINKING IT OVER:

    For Senior Students 177

    Simpler Exercises 193

    Further Reading 199

    A Note for Amateur Dramatic Societies . 201

APPENDIX: Extracts from the First Quarto
Hamlet 203

INTRODUCTION

" 'FAITH, it should please all, like Prince Hamlet," wrote Anthony Scoloker in 1604, and so became unconsciously a prophet. For over three hundred years *Hamlet* has held the English stage, and in our own time has been often acclaimed by peoples beyond the ken of those Elizabethans who applauded it so heartily at the Globe Theatre. It has been acted in twenty languages or more, from Tokio to New York, from Australia to Iceland, and during 1928 there were over ninety performances in German in the theatres of Central Europe. It has established itself as the most popular of Shakespeare's plays with the theatre-going public, and the most typical of his poetic genius ; while scholars continue to discuss its problems, our great tragic actors aspire to the title-rôle, and many of its phrases have been woven into the texture of our daily speech, their origin half-forgotten.

A play so universally popular needs little introduction. It makes its own appeal through the interest of plot and characters, a story of murder and treachery and revenge, with all their tragic implications shown to the full, which ends suddenly and terribly in a duel and death.

There is no political situation to be explained or historical setting to be described. Hamlet belongs to all time. We can picture him if we choose at the court of eleventh-century Denmark, living in a half-savage world ; but that the barbarities of the play do not make it merely a thing of the past the history of the years 1914–1918 bears terrible witness. Recently the whole drama has been successfully staged in modern dress, with only some minor points of thought and action, some details of " the outward habit of encounter," that seemed incongruous with a Hamlet in plus fours or an Ophelia in a Parisian gown. Shakespeare's company always acted the play in " modern dress."

There is much to be said, however, in favour of the mediæval setting which is usual on the modern stage for this and a number of other Shakespearean plays, for the trappings of *Hamlet* are mediæval. So we may build for ourselves, in the theatres of our own minds, the grey stone battlements of Elsinore and the wide, gloomy chambers, hung with tapestry, strewn with rushes, of a palace which is more than half fortress. Here the younger men of the play appear in short tunic, long hose, and pointed shoes, ranging in richness and colour from Hamlet's " customary suit of solemn black " to the foppish dress of Osric, jewelled and trimmed with fur. The King and Polonius have long tunics falling well below the knee, and over these heavy, rich gowns with wide sleeves hanging loose; and on his first appearance the King wears a wide, jewelled belt and a jewelled crown. The Queen and Ophelia appear in long flowing dresses, made in one piece, with close-fitting sleeves which reach the wrist and a girdle tied in front, its ends hanging almost to the ground. Over their neck and shoulders falls a loose head-dress, under which their long hair is gathered up. The grave-diggers wear rough brown jerkins. The players are dressed like the courtiers, but less richly, their clothes faded and travel-worn. The sentinels wear the helmet and breastplate of men-at-arms, and they are keeping their nervous watch, pike in hand, upon the dark battlements of Elsinore when the curtain rises upon the first act of the tragedy.

DRAMATIS PERSONÆ

CLAUDIUS, *King of Denmark.*
HAMLET, *son to the late, and nephew to the present king.*
POLONIUS, *Lord Chamberlain.*
HORATIO, *friend to Hamlet.*
LAERTES, *son to Polonius.*
VOLTIMAND,
CORNELIUS,
ROSENCRANTZ,
GUILDENSTERN, } *courtiers.*
OSRIC,
A Gentleman,
A Priest.
MARCELLUS, } *officers.*
BERNARDO,
FRANCISCO, *a soldier.*
REYNALDO, *servant to Polonius.*
Players.
Two Clowns, *grave-diggers.*
FORTINBRAS, *Prince of Norway.*
A Captain.
English Ambassadors.

GERTRUDE, *Queen of Denmark, and mother to Hamlet.*
OPHELIA, *daughter to Polonius.*

Lords, Ladies, Officers, Soldiers, Sailors, Messengers, and other Attendants.
Ghost of Hamlet's Father.

Scene : Denmark.

The text is that of the *Globe Shakespeare* (with slight omissions), here reprinted by kind permission of Messrs. Macmillan and Co. A number of stage-directions have been added.
In most cases of disputed meanings the Oxford *Shakespeare Glossary* has been followed.

HAMLET,
PRINCE OF DENMARK

ACT I

SCENE I

*The battlements of Elsinore. It is past midnight,
bitterly cold, and dark except for the faint light of the
stars.*

*Francisco is on guard. His relief, Bernardo, enters
along the battlements, and, coming upon him suddenly, is
startled into challenging him. Both speak in low voices
which betray their nervous tension.*

Bernardo. Who's there ?

Francisco. Nay, answer *me* : stand, and unfold
    yourself.

Bernardo [*giving the pass-word*]. Long live the
    king !

Francisco [*anxiously peering at him*]. Bernardo ?

Bernardo. He.

Francisco [*relieved*]. You come most carefully upon
    your hour.

Bernardo. 'Tis now struck twelve ; get thee to bed,
    Francisco.

Francisco. For this relief much thanks : 'tis bitter
    cold,
And I am sick at heart.

10 *Bernardo.* Have you had quiet guard ?
 Francisco.   Not a mouse stirring.
 Bernardo. Well, good night.
If you do meet Horatio and Marcellus,
The rivals of my watch, bid them make haste.
 Francisco. I think I hear them. Stand, ho ! Who's
     there ?

          [*Enter Horatio and Marcellus.*]
 Horatio. Friends to this ground.
 Marcellus.   And liegemen to the Dane.
 Francisco. Give you good night.
 Marcellus.   O, farewell, honest soldier :
Who hath relieved you ?
 Francisco.   Bernardo has my place.
Give you good night.   [*Exit.*]
 Marcellus.   Holla ! Bernardo !
 Bernardo.   Say,
What, is Horatio there ?
 Horatio.   .   A piece of him.
20 *Bernardo.* Welcome, Horatio : welcome, good Mar-
     cellus.
 Marcellus. What, has this Thing appear'd again
     to-night ?
 Bernardo.. I have seen nothing.
 Marcellus. Horatio says 'tis but our fantasy,
And will not let belief take hold of him
Touching this dreaded sight, twice seen of us :
Therefore I have entreated him along
With us to watch the minutes of this night ;.
That if again this apparition come,
He may approve our eyes and speak to it.
30 *Horatio.* Tush, tush, 'twill not appear.
 Bernardo.   Sit down awhile ;
And let us once again assail your ears,
That are so fortified against our story
What we have two nights seen.

                13. *Rivals*, Partners.
                     12

Horatio.   Well, sit we down,
And let us hear Bernardo speak of this.

Bernardo. Last night of all,
When yond same star that's westward from the pole
Had made his course to illume that part of heaven
Where now it burns, Marcellus and myself,
The bell then beating one,—

                    [*The Ghost appears.*]

40 *Marcellus.* Peace, break thee off; look, where it
        comes again!

Bernardo. In the same figure, like the king that's
        dead.

Marcellus. Thou art a scholar; speak to it,
        Horatio.

Bernardo. Looks it not like the king? mark it,
        Horatio.

Horatio. Most like: it harrows me with fear and
        wonder.

Bernardo. It would be spoke to.

Marcellus.   Question it, Horatio.

Horatio. What art thou that usurp'st this time of
        night,
Together with that fair and warlike form
In which the majesty of buried Denmark
Did sometimes march? By heaven I charge thee,
        speak!

50 *Marcellus.* It is offended.

Bernardo.   See, it stalks away!

Horatio. Stay! speak, speak! I charge thee, speak!
                    [*The Ghost vanishes.*]

Marcellus. 'Tis gone, and will not answer.

Bernardo. How now, Horatio! you tremble and
        look pale:
Is not this something more than fantasy?

---

41. *The king that's dead,* Prince Hamlet's father, who has died
    recently in mysterious circumstances: *the majesty of buried
    Denmark* (48).
54. *Fantasy,* Imagination.

13

What think you on't?

Horatio. Before my God, I might not this believe
Without the sensible and true avouch
Of mine own eyes.

 Marcellus.   Is it not like the king?

 Horatio. As thou art to thyself:
60 Such was the very armour he had on
When he the ambitious Norway combated;
So frown'd he once, when, in an angry parle,
He smote the sledded Polacks on the ice.
'Tis strange.

 Marcellus. Thus twice before, and jump at this
    dead hour,
With martial stalk hath he gone by our watch.

 Horatio. In what particular thought to work I know
   not;
But in the gross and scope of my opinion,
This bodes some strange eruption to our state.

70 *Marcellus.* Good now, sit down, and tell me, he
   that knows
Why this same strict and most observant watch
So nightly toils the subject of the land,
And why such daily cast of brazen cannon,
And foreign mart for implements of war;
Why such impress of shipwrights, whose sore task
Does not divide the Sunday from the week;
What might be toward, that this sweaty haste
Doth make the night joint-labourer with the day:
Who is't that can inform me?

 Horatio.   That can I;
80 At least, the whisper goes so. Our last king,
Whose image even but now appear'd to us,
Was, as you know, by Fortinbras of Norway,
Thereto prick'd on by a most emulate pride,
Dared to the combat; in which our valiant Hamlet—

---

57. *Sensible*, Evident to the senses.   62. *Parle*, Parley.
63. *Sledded Polacks*, Polish warriors in sledges.
65. *Jump*, Exactly.

For so this side of our known world esteem'd him—
Did slay this Fortinbras ; who, by a seal'd compact,
Well ratified by law and heraldry,
Did forfeit, with his life, all those his lands
Which he stood seized of, to the conqueror :
90 Against the which, a moiety competent
Was gaged by our king ; which had return'd
To the inheritance of Fortinbras,
Had he been vanquisher ; as, by the same covenant,
And carriage of the article design'd,
His fell to Hamlet.   Now, sir, young Fortinbras,
Of unimproved mettle hot and full,
Hath in the skirts of Norway here and there
Shark'd up a list of lawless resolutes,
For food and diet, to some enterprise
100 That hath a stomach in't ; which is no other—
As it doth well appear unto our state—
But to recover of us, by strong hand
And terms compulsatory, those foresaid lands
So by his father lost : and this, I take it,
Is the main motive of our preparations,
The source of this our watch, and the chief head
Of this post-haste and romage in the land.
    Bernardo.   I think it be no other but e'en so :
Well may it sort that this portentous figure
110 Comes armed through our watch ; so like the king
That was and is the question of these wars.
    Horatio.   A mote it is to trouble the mind's eye.
In the most high and palmy state of Rome,
A little ere the mightiest Julius fell,
The graves stood tenantless and the sheeted dead
Did squeak and gibber in the Roman streets :
As stars with trains of fire and dews of blood,

89. *Seized of,* Possessed.
90. *Moiety competent,* Equivalent portion.
96. *Unimproved,* Unproved, not put to use.
98. *Shark'd up,* Got together at haphazard (contemptuous).
98. *List . . . resolutes,* Band of desperadoes.
100. *Hath a stomach in't,* Risky (stomach=courage).

Disasters in the sun ; and the moist star
Upon whose influence Neptune's empire stands
120 Was sick almost to doomsday with eclipse :
And even the like precurse of fierce events,
As harbingers preceding still the fates
And prologue to the omen coming on,
Have heaven and earth together demonstrated
Unto our climatures and countrymen.—
But soft, behold ! lo, where it comes again !
                        [*The Ghost appears.*]
I'll cross it, though it blast me.   Stay, illusion !
If thou hast any sound, or use of voice,
Speak to me :
130 If there be any good thing to be done,
That may to thee do ease and grace to me,
Speak to me :   [*Cock crows.*]
If thou art privy to thy country's fate,
Which, happily, foreknowing may avoid,
O, speak !
Or if thou hast uphoarded in thy life
Extorted treasure in the womb of earth,
For which, they say, you spirits oft walk in death,
Speak of it : stay, and speak !   Stop it, Marcellus.
140   *Marcellus.* Shall I strike at it with my partisan ?
    Horatio. Do, if it will not stand.
    Bernardo.   'Tis here !
    Horatio.   'Tis here !
    Marcellus. 'Tis gone !   [*The Ghost vanishes.*]
We do it wrong, being so majestical,
To offer it the show of violence ;
For it is, as the air, invulnerable,
And our vain blows malicious mockery.
    Bernardo. It was about to speak, when the cock
        crew.
    Horatio. And then it started like a guilty thing

118. *Moist star,* Moon, which governs the tides of the sea : *Neptune's*
    empire.   121. *Precurse,* Forerunner.
125. *Climatures,* Regions (?).   140. *Partisan,* Halberd, pike.
    (3,362)   16

Upon a fearful summons. I have heard,
150 The cock, that is the trumpet to the morn,
Doth with his lofty and shrill-sounding throat
Awake the god of day ; and, at his warning,
Whether in sea or fire, in earth or air,
The extravagant and erring spirit hies
To his confine : and of the truth herein
This present object made probation.
    Marcellus. It faded on the crowing of the cock.
Some say that ever 'gainst that season comes
Wherein our Saviour's birth is celebrated,
160 The bird of dawning singeth all night long :
And then, they say, no spirit dare stir abroad ;
The nights are wholesome ; then no planets strike,
No fairy takes, nor witch hath power to charm,
So hallow'd and so gracious is the time.
    Horatio. So have I heard and do in part be-
    lieve it.
But, look, the morn, in russet mantle clad,
Walks o'er the dew of yon high eastward hill :
Break we our watch up ; and by my advice,
Let us impart what we have seen to-night
170 Unto young Hamlet ; for, upon my life,
This spirit, dumb to us, will speak to him.
Do you consent we shall acquaint him with it,
As needful in our loves, fitting our duty ?
    Marcellus. Let's do't, I pray ; and I this morning
    know
Where we shall find him most conveniently.

                                [Exeunt.]

---

154. *Extravagant and erring*, Spirit which has wandered out of its
    bounds.
162. *Planets strike*, Exert evil influence on human beings. It was
    long believed that the motions of the stars controlled human
    destinies.
163. *Fairy takes*, Smites with disease.

SCENE II

The throne-room of the Castle of Elsinore. There is a flourish of trumpets. Enter in state the King, the Queen, Polonius, Laertes; Voltimand and Cornelius, the Ambassadors to Norway; Lords and Attendants; and Hamlet. His mourning-suit of black is in striking contrast with the rich, gay dresses of the others.

The King and Queen ascend the steps of the throne, and all the others group themselves about the room with an air of respectful attention—except Hamlet, who takes a seat as far as possible from the throne and appears to be lost in gloomy meditation. The Queen sits. The King turns to face the assembly, and surveys them for a moment before he begins his speech.

King. Though yet of Hamlet our dear brother's
　　death
The memory be green, and that it us befitted
To bear our hearts in grief and our whole kingdom
To be contracted in one brow of woe,
Yet so far hath discretion fought with nature
That we with wisest sorrow think on him,
Together with remembrance of ourselves.
Therefore our sometime sister, now our queen,
The imperial jointress to this warlike state,
10 Have we, as 'twere with a defeated joy,—
With an auspicious and a dropping eye,
With mirth in funeral and with dirge in marriage,
In equal scale weighing delight and dole,—
Taken to wife : nor have we herein barr'd
Your better wisdoms, which have freely gone
With this affair along.　For all, our thanks.
Now follows, that you know, young Fortinbras,

8. *Our sometime sister.* Claudius has married his brother's widow
　—a month after his brother's death.　　13. *Dole*, Grief.

Holding a weak supposal of our worth,
Or thinking by our late dear brother's death
20 Our state to be disjoint and out of frame,
Colleagued with the dream of his advantage,
He hath not fail'd to pester us with message,
Importing the surrender of those lands
Lost by his father, with all bonds of law,
To our most valiant brother.   So much for him.
Now for ourself and for this time of meeting :
Thus much the business is : we have here writ
To Norway, uncle of young Fortinbras,—
Who, impotent and bed-rid, scarcely hears
30 Of this his nephew's purpose,—to suppress
His further gait herein ; in that the levies,
The lists and full proportions, are all made
Out of his subject : and we here dispatch
You, good Cornelius, and you, Voltimand,
For bearers of this greeting to old Norway ;
Giving to you no further personal power
To business with the king, more than the scope
Of these delated articles allow.
Farewell, and let your haste commend your duty.
40   *Cornelius.* }   In that and all things will we show
      Voltimand. }   our duty.
        King. We doubt it nothing : heartily farewell.
                        [*Exeunt Voltimand and Cornelius.*]
And now, Laertes, what's the news with you ?
You told us of some suit ; what is't, Laertes ?
You cannot speak of reason to the Dane,
And lose your voice : what wouldst thou beg, Laertes,
That shall not be my offer, not thy asking ?
The head is not more native to the heart,
The hand more instrumental to the mouth,
Than is the throne of Denmark to thy father.
50 What wouldst thou have, Laertes ?
        Laertes.   My dread lord,

21. *Colleagued*, United.   31. *Gait*, Course.
        38. *Delated*, Expressly stated (?).

Your leave and favour to return to France ;
From whence though willingly I came to Denmark,
To show my duty in your coronation,
Yet now, I must confess, that duty done,
My thoughts and wishes bend again toward France
And bow them to your gracious leave and pardon.

  King. Have you your father's leave ? What says
   Polonius ?
  Polonius. He hath, my lord, wrung from me my
   slow leave
By laboursome petition, and at last
60 Upon his will I seal'd my hard consent :
I do beseech you, give him leave to go.
  King. Take thy fair hour, Laertes ; time be thine,
And thy best graces spend it at thy will !
But now, my cousin Hamlet, and my son,—
  Hamlet [*aside*]. A little more than kin, and less than
   kind.
  King. How is it that the clouds still hang on you ?
  Hamlet. Not so, my lord ; I am too much i' the sun.
  Queen. Good Hamlet, cast thy nighted colour off,
And let thine eye look like a friend on Denmark.
70 Do not for ever with thy vailed lids
Seek for thy noble father in the dust :
Thou know'st 'tis common ; all that lives must die,
Passing through nature to eternity.
  Hamlet. Ay, madam, it is common.
  Queen.   If it be,
Why seems it so particular with thee ?
  Hamlet. Seems, madam ! nay, it is ; I know not
   " seems."
'Tis not alone my inky cloak, good mother,
Nor customary suits of solemn black,
Nor windy suspiration of forced breath,
80 No, nor the fruitful river in the eye,
Nor the dejected 'haviour of the visage,

   65. *Kind,* Natural.   67. *I' the sun,* homeless (?).
       70. *Vailed,* Lowered.

Together with all forms, moods, shapes of grief,
That can denote me truly : these indeed seem,
For they are actions that a man might play :
But I have that within which passeth show ;
These but the trappings and the suits of woe.
 King. 'Tis sweet and commendable in your nature,
  Hamlet,
To give these mourning duties to your father :
But, you must know, your father lost a father ;
90 That father lost, lost his, and the survivor bound
In filial obligation for some term
To do obsequious sorrow : but to persever
In obstinate condolement is a course
Of impious stubbornness ; 'tis unmanly grief ;
It shows a will most incorrect to heaven,
A heart unfortified, a mind impatient,
An understanding simple and unschool'd :
For what we know must be and is as common
As any the most vulgar thing to sense,
100 Why should we in our peevish opposition
Take it to heart ?　Fie ! 'tis a fault to heaven,
A fault against the dead, a fault to nature,
To reason most absurd ; whose common theme
Is death of fathers, and who still hath cried,
From the first corse till he that died to-day,
" This must be so."　We pray you, throw to earth
This unprevailing woe, and think of us
As of a father : for let the world take note,
You are the most immediate to our throne ;
110 And with no less nobility of love
Than that which dearest father bears his son,
Do I impart toward you.　For your intent
In going back to school in Wittenberg,
It is most retrograde to our desire :
And we beseech you, bend you to remain
Here, in the cheer and comfort of our eye,

97. *Simple,* Foolish.   **107.** *Unprevailing,* Unavailing.
     114. *Retrograde,* Contrary.

Our chiefest courtier, cousin, and our son.

    Queen. Let not thy mother lose her prayers,
        Hamlet :
I pray thee, stay with us ; go not to Wittenberg.
120   *Hamlet.* I shall in all my best obey you, madam.
    King. Why, 'tis a loving and a fair reply :
Be as ourself in Denmark.   Madam, come ;
This gentle and unforced accord of Hamlet
Sits smiling to my heart : in grace whereof,
No jocund health that Denmark drinks to-day,
But the great cannon to the clouds shall tell,
And the king's rouse the heavens shall bruit again,
Re-speaking earthly thunder.   Come away.
                 [Exeunt all but Hamlet.]

    Hamlet. O, that this too too solid flesh would
        melt,
130 Thaw and resolve itself into a dew !
Or that the everlasting had not fix'd
His canon 'gainst self-slaughter !   O God ! God !
How weary, stale, flat and unprofitable,
Seem to me all the uses of this world !
Fie on't ! ah fie ! 'tis an unweeded garden,
That grows to seed ; things rank and gross in nature
Possess it merely.   That it should come to this !
But two months dead : nay, not so much, not two :
So excellent a king ; that was, to this,
140 Hyperion to a satyr ; so loving to my mother
That he might not beteem the winds of heaven
Visit her face too roughly.   Heaven and earth !
Must I remember ? why, she would hang on him,
As if increase of appetite had grown
By what it fed on : and yet, within a month—
Let me not think on't—Frailty, thy name is
    woman !—

---

117. *Cousin.* Often used of nephew, niece, uncle, etc., in Eliza-
    bethan English.
140. *Hyperion to a satyr.* As the beautiful sun-god is to a bestial
    creature.   141. *Beteem,* Allow.

A little month, or ere those shoes were old
With which she follow'd my poor father's body,
Like Niobe, all tears :—why she, even she—
150 O God ! a beast, that wants discourse of reason,
Would have mourn'd longer—married with my
  uncle,
My father's brother, but no more like my father
Than I to Hercules : within a month :
Ere yet the salt of most unrighteous tears
Had left the flushing in her galled eyes,
She married.   O, most wicked speed.
It is not nor it cannot come to good :
But break, my heart ; for I must hold my tongue.

    [Enter Horatio, Marcellus, and Bernardo.]

160   *Horatio.* Hail to your lordship !
    Hamlet.   I am glad to see you well :
Horatio,—or I do forget myself.
   Horatio. The same, my lord, and your poor servant
  ever.
   Hamlet. Sir, my good friend ; I'll change that name
  with you :
And what make you from Wittenberg, Horatio ?
Marcellus ?
   Marcellus. My good lord—
   Hamlet. I am very glad to see you.   Good even,
  sir.
But what, in faith, make you from Wittenberg ?
   Horatio. A truant disposition, good my lord.
170   *Hamlet.* I would not hear your enemy say so.
Nor shall you do mine ear that violence,
To make it truster of your own report
Against yourself : I know you are no truant.
But what is your affair in Elsinore ?
We'll teach you to drink deep ere you depart.
   Horatio. My lord, I came to see your father's fun-
  eral.

149. *Niobe* wept ceaselessly for the death of her children.
153. *Hercules,* The Greek hero famous for his great physical strength.

23

Hamlet. I pray thee, do not mock me, fellow-
　　student ;
I think it was to see my mother's wedding.
　Horatio. Indeed, my lord, it follow'd hard upon.
180　*Hamlet.* Thrift, thrift, Horatio ! the funeral baked-
　　meats
Did coldly furnish forth the marriage tables.
Would I had met my dearest foe in heaven
Or ever I had seen that day, Horatio !
My father !—methinks I see my father.
　Horatio. Where, my lord ?
　Hamlet.　　　　　　　　In my mind's eye, Horatio.
　Horatio. I saw him once ; he was a goodly king.
　Hamlet. He was a man, take him for all in all,
I shall not look upon his like again.
　Horatio. My lord, I think I saw him yesternight.
190　*Hamlet.* Saw ? who ?
　Horatio. My lord, the king your father.
　Hamlet.　　　　　　　　　The king my father !
　Horatio. Season your admiration for a while
With an attent ear, till I may deliver,
Upon the witness of these gentlemen,
This marvel to you.
　Hamlet.　　　　　For God's love, let me hear.
　Horatio. Two nights together had these gentlemen,
Marcellus and Bernardo, on their watch,
In the dead vast and middle of the night,
Been thus encounter'd.　A figure like your father,
200 Armed at point exactly, cap-a-pe,
Appears before them, and with solemn march
Goes slow and stately by them : thrice he walk'd
By their oppress'd and fear-surprised eyes,
Within his truncheon's length ; whilst they, distill'd
Almost to jelly with the act of fear,

180. *Baked-meats*, Pastry.
192. *Season your admiration*, Modify your astonishment.
200. *At point exactly, cap-a-pe*, Completely armed, from head to
　　foot.

Stand dumb and speak not to him.   This to me
In dreadful secrecy impart they did ;
And I with them the third night kept the watch :
Where, as they had deliver'd, both in time,
210 Form of the thing, each word made true and good,
The apparition comes : I knew your father ;
These hands are not more like.

  Hamlet.   But where was this ?
  Marcellus. My lord, upon the platform where we
    watch'd.
  Hamlet. Did you not speak to it ?
  Horatio.   My lord, I did ;
But answer made it none : yet once methought
It lifted up it head and did address
Itself to motion, like as it would speak ;
But even then the morning cock crew loud,
And at the sound it shrunk in haste away,
220 And vanish'd from our sight.

  Hamlet.   'Tis very strange.
  Horatio. As I do live, my honour'd lord, 'tis true ;
And we did think it writ down in our duty
To let you know of it.
  Hamlet. Indeed, indeed, sirs, but this troubles me.
Hold you the watch to-night ?

  Marcellus. }
  Bernardo. }   We do, my lord.
  Hamlet. Arm'd, say you ?
  Marcellus. }
  Bernardo. } Arm'd, my lord.
  Hamlet. From top to toe ?
  Marcellus. }
  Bernardo. } My lord, from head to foot.
  Hamlet. Then saw you not his face ?
230 *Horatio.* O, yes, my lord ; he wore his beaver up.
  Hamlet. What, look'd he frowningly ?
  Horatio. A countenance more in sorrow than in anger.

---

230. *Beaver*, Vizor, movable part of the helmet which covered the
  face.

Hamlet. Pale or red ?

Horatio. Nay, very pale.

Hamlet.   And fix'd his eyes upon you ?

Horatio. Most constantly.

Hamlet.   I would I had been there.

Horatio. It would have much amazed you.

Hamlet. Very like, very like.   Stay'd it long ?

Horatio. While one with moderate haste might tell
   a hundred.

Marcellus. ⎱
Bernardo. ⎰ Longer, longer.

240 *Horatio.* Not when I saw 't.

Hamlet.   His beard was grizzled—no ?

Horatio. It was, as I have seen it in his life,
A sable silver'd.

Hamlet.   I will watch to-night ;
Perchance 'twill walk again.

Horatio.   I warrant it will.

Hamlet. If it assume my noble father's person,
I'll speak to it, though hell itself should gape
And bid me hold my peace.   I pray you all,
If you have hitherto conceal'd this sight,
Let it be tenable in your silence still ;
And whatsoever else shall hap to-night,
250 Give it an understanding, but no tongue :
I will requite your loves.   So, fare you well :
Upon the platform, 'twixt eleven and twelve,
I'll visit you.

All.   Our duty to your honour.

Hamlet. Your loves, as mine to you : farewell.

                         [*Exeunt all but Hamlet.*]
My father's spirit in arms ! all is not well ;
I doubt some foul play : would the night were come !
Till then sit still, my soul : foul deeds will rise,
Though all the earth o'erwhelm them, to men's eyes.

                                        [*Exit.*]

---

238. *Tell*, Count.   240. *Grizzled*, Grey.

242. *Sable*, Black.

26

SCENE III

A room in Polonius' house.

[*Enter Laertes and Ophelia.*]
Laertes. My necessaries are embark'd : farewell :
And, sister, as the winds give benefit
And convoy is assistant, do not sleep,
But let me hear from you.
    Ophelia.   Do you doubt that ?
Laertes. For Hamlet and the trifling of his favour,
Hold it a fashion and a toy in blood,
A violet in the youth of primy nature,
Forward, not permanent, sweet, not lasting,
The perfume and suppliance of a minute ;
10 No more.
    Ophelia. No more but so ?
    Laertes.   Think it no more :
For nature, crescent, does not grow alone
In thews and bulk, but, as this temple waxes,
The inward service of the mind and soul
Grows wide withal.   Perhaps he loves you now,
And now no soil nor cautel doth besmirch
The virtue of his will : but you must fear,
His greatness weigh'd, his will is not his own ;
For he himself is subject to his birth : ·
He may not, as unvalued persons do,
20 Carve for himself ; for on his choice depends
The safety and health of this whole state ;
And therefore must his choice be circumscribed
Unto the voice and yielding of that body
Whereof he is the head.   Then if he says he loves you,
It fits your wisdom so far to believe it

3. *Convoy is assistant*, Means of conveyance are available.
7. *Primy*, Spring-time.   9. *Suppliance*, Diversion.
11. *Crescent*, Growing.   15. *Cautel*, Crafty device, trickery.

As he in his particular **act** and place
May give his saying deed ; which is no further
Than the main voice of Denmark goes withal.
Then weigh what loss your honour may sustain,
30 If with too credent ear you list his songs,
Or lose your heart.
Fear it, Ophelia, fear it, my dear sister,
And keep you in the rear of your affection,
Out of the shot and danger of desire.
The chariest maid is prodigal enough,
If she unmask her beauty to the moon :
Virtue itself 'scapes not calumnious strokes :
The canker galls the infants of the spring,
Too oft before their buttons be disclosed,
40 And in the morn and liquid dew of youth
Contagious blastments are most imminent.
Be wary then ; best safety lies in fear :
Youth to itself rebels, though none else near.
   Ophelia. I shall the effect of this good lesson keep,
As watchman to my heart.   But, good my brother,
Do not, as some ungracious pastors do,
Show me the steep and thorny way to heaven ;
Whiles, like a puff'd and reckless libertine,
Himself the primrose path of dalliance treads,
50 And recks not his own rede.
   Laertes.   O, fear me not.
I stay too long : but here my father comes.
                [*Enter Polonius.*]
A double blessing is a double grace ;
Occasion smiles upon a second leave.
   Polonius. Yet here, Laertes ! aboard, aboard, for
         shame !
The wind sits in the shoulder of your sail,
And you are stay'd for.   There ; my blessing with
         thee !
And these few precepts in thy memory

30. *Credent*, Trustful.   39. *Buttons*, Buds.   *Disclosed*, Opened.
50. *Recks not his own rede*, Does not follow his own advice.

See thou character.   Give thy thoughts no tongue,
Nor any unproportion'd thought his act.
60 Be thou familiar, but by no means vulgar.
Those friends thou hast, and their adoption tried,
Grapple them to thy soul with hoops of steel ;
But do not dull thy palm with entertainment
Of each new-hatch'd, unfledged comrade.   Beware
Of entrance to a quarrel, but being in,
Bear 't that the opposed may beware of thee.
Give every man thy ear, but few thy voice ;
Take each man's censure, but reserve thy judgment.
Costly thy habit as thy purse can buy,
70 But not express'd in fancy ; rich, not gaudy ;
For the apparel oft proclaims the man,
And they in France of the best rank and station
Are of a most select and generous chief in that.
Neither a borrower nor a lender be ;
For loan oft loses both itself and friend,
And borrowing dulls the edge of husbandry.
This above all : to thine own self be true,
And it must follow, as the night the day,
Thou canst not then be false to any man.
80 Farewell : my blessing season this in thee !
 Laertes. Most humbly do I take my leave, my lord.
 Polonius. The time invites you ; go ; your servants
  tend.
 Laertes. Farewell, Ophelia ; and remember well
What I have said to you.
 Ophelia.   'Tis in my memory lock'd,
And you yourself shall keep the key of it.
 Laertes. Farewell.   [*Exit.*]
 Polonius. What is 't, Ophelia, he hath said to you ?
 Ophelia. So please you, something touching the Lord
  Hamlet.

58. *Character,* Engrave, inscribe.   68. *Censure,* Opinion.
70. *Express'd in fancy,* Fantastic.
73. *Chief,* Eminence (?).
76. *Husbandry,* Thrift.   80. *Season,* Mature.
82. *Tend,* Wait.

Polonius. Marry, well bethought :
90 'Tis told me, he hath very oft of late
Given private time to you ; and you yourself
Have of your audience been most free and bounteous :
If it be so, as so 'tis put on me,
And that in way of caution, I must tell you,
You do not understand yourself so clearly
As it behoves my daughter and your honour.
What is between you ? give me up the truth.
    Ophelia. He hath, my lord, of late made many tenders
Of his affection to me.
100   *Polonius.* Affection ! pooh ! you speak like a green girl,
Unsifted in such perilous circumstance.
Do you believe his tenders, as you call them ?
    Ophelia. I do not know, my lord, what I should think.
    Polonius. Marry, I'll teach you : think yourself a baby ;
That you have ta'en these tenders for true pay,
Which are not sterling.   Tender yourself more dearly ;
Or—not to crack the wind of the poor phrase,
Running it thus—you'll tender me a fool.
    Ophelia. My lord, he hath importuned me with love
110 In honourable fashion.
    Polonius. Ay, fashion you may call it ; go to, go to.
    Ophelia. And hath given countenance to his speech, my lord,
With almost all the holy vows of heaven.
    Polonius. Ay, springes to catch woodcocks.   I do know,
When the blood burns, how prodigal the soul
Lends the tongue vows : these blazes, daughter,

89. *Marry*, A petty oath ; from the Virgin Mary.
98. *Tenders*, Offers.   106. *Tender yourself*, Take care of yourself.
110. *Fashion*, Manner.   111. *Fashion*, Pretence.
114. *Springes*, Traps.   *Woodcocks* are regarded as stupid birds.

Giving more light than heat, extinct in both,
Even in their promise, as it is a-making,
You must not take for fire. From this time
120 Be somewhat scanter of your maiden presence ;
Set your entreatments at a higher rate
Than a command to parley. For Lord Hamlet,
Believe so much in him, that he is young,
And with a larger tether may he walk
Than may be given you : in few, Ophelia,
Do not believe his vows ; for they are brokers,
Not of that dye which their investments show,
But mere implorators of unholy suits,
Breathing like sanctified and pious bonds,
130 The better to beguile. This is for all :
I would not, in plain terms, from this time forth,
Have you so slander any moment leisure,
As to give words or talk with the Lord Hamlet.
Look to 't, I charge you : come your ways.
   Ophelia. I shall obey, my lord.   *[Exeunt.]*

SCENE IV

The battlements of the castle.

   [Enter Hamlet, Horatio, and Marcellus.]
Hamlet. The air bites shrewdly ; it is very cold.
Horatio. It is a nipping and an eager air.
Hamlet. What hour now ?
Horatio.   I think it lacks of twelve.
Marcellus. No, it is struck.
Horatio. Indeed ? I heard it not : then it draws
    near the season
Wherein the spirit held his wont to walk.
   [A flourish of trumpets, and ordnance shot off,
     within.]
   Horatio. What does this mean, my lord ?

127. *Investments,* Dresses.   129. *Bonds,* Legal documents.

Hamlet. The king doth wake to-night and takes his
  rouse,
Keeps wassail, and the swaggering up-spring reels ;
10 And, as he drains his draughts of Rhenish down,
The kettle-drum and trumpet thus bray out
The triumph of his pledge.
 Horatio.   Is it a custom ?
 Hamlet. Ay, marry, is't :
But to my mind, though I am native here
And to the manner born, it is a custom
More honour'd in the breach than the observance.
This heavy-headed revel east and west
Makes us traduced and tax'd of other nations :
They clepe us drunkards, and with swinish phrase
20 Soil our addition ; and indeed it takes
From our achievements, though perform'd at height
The pith and marrow of our attribute.
So, oft it chances in particular men,
That for some vicious mole of nature in them,
As, in their birth—wherein they are not guilty,
Since nature cannot choose his origin—
By the o'ergrowth of some complexion,
Oft breaking down the pales and forts of reason,
Or by some habit that too much o'er-leavens
30 The form of plausive manners, that these men,
Carrying, I say, the stamp of one defect,
Being nature's livery, or fortune's star,—
Their virtues else—be they as pure as grace,
As infinite as man may undergo—
Shall in the general censure take corruption
From that particular fault : the dram of eale
Doth all the noble substance of a doubt
To his own scandal.

---

8. *Wake,* Revel. *Rouse,* Full draught of liquor.
9. *Wassail,* Drinking-bout. *Up-spring reels,* Wild dances.
18. *Tax'd,* Censured.   19. *Clepe,* Call.
20. *Addition,* Title, style of address.
22. *Attribute,* Reputation.   30. *Plausive,* Pleasing.
36. *Eale,* evil (?). A very difficult passage. See page 148.

Horatio.   Look, my lord, it comes !
                    [*The Ghost appears.*]
    Hamlet. Angels and ministers of grace defend us !
40 Be thou a spirit of health or goblin damn'd,
    Bring with thee airs from heaven or blasts from hell,
    Be thy intents wicked or charitable,
    Thou comest in such a questionable shape
    That I will speak to thee : I'll call thee Hamlet,
    King, father, royal Dane : O, answer me !
    Let me not burst in ignorance ; but tell
    Why thy canonized bones, hearsed in death,
    Have burst their cerements : why the sepulchre,
    Wherein we saw thee quietly inurn'd,
50 Hath oped his ponderous and marble jaws,
    To cast thee up again.   What may this mean,
    That thou, dead corse, again in complete steel
    Revisit'st thus the glimpses of the moon,
    Making night hideous ; and we fools of nature
    So horridly to shake our disposition
    With thoughts beyond the reaches of our souls ?
    Say, why is this ? wherefore ? what should we do ?
                         [*The Ghost beckons Hamlet.*]
    Horatio. It beckons you to go away with it,
    As if it some impartment did desire
60 To you alone.
        Marcellus.   Look, with what courteous action
    It waves you to a more removed ground :
    But do not go with it.
        Horatio.   No, by no means.
    Hamlet. It will not speak ; then I will follow it.
    Horatio. Do not, my lord.
    Hamlet.   Why, what should be the fear ?
    I do not set my life at a pin's fee ;
    And for my soul, what can it do to that,
    Being a thing immortal as itself ?

    47. *Canonized*, Buried with Church rites.
    48. *Cerements*, Grave-clothes.
    54. *Fools of nature*, Barred by nature from knowledge of the
        supernatural.

It waves me forth again : I'll follow it.

    Horatio. What if it tempt you toward the flood, my
        lord,
70 Or to the dreadful summit of the cliff
That beetles o'er his base into the sea,
And there assume some other horrible form,
Which might deprive your sovereignty of reason
And draw you into madness ? Think of it :
The very place puts toys of desperation,
Without more motive, into every brain
That looks so many fathoms to the sea
And hears it roar beneath.

    Hamlet.   It waves me still.
Go on ; I'll follow thee.
80   *Marcellus.* You shall not go, my lord.

    Hamlet.   Hold off your hands.

    Horatio. Be ruled ; you shall not go.

    Hamlet.   My fate cries out,
And makes each petty artery in this body
As hardy as the Nemean lion's nerve.
Still am I call'd. Unhand me, gentlemen.
By heaven, I'll make a ghost of him that lets me !—
[*Breaking away from them he turns to the Ghost*] I say,
    away ! Go on ; I'll follow thee.
        [*He follows the Ghost along the battlements*.]

    Horatio. He waxes desperate with imagination.

    Marcellus. Let's follow ; 'tis not fit thus to obey
        him.

    Horatio. Have after. To what issue will this come ?
90   *Marcellus.* Something is rotten in the state of Den-
        mark.

    Horatio. Heaven will direct it.

    Marcellus.   Nay, let's follow him.
                        [*Exeunt.*]

---

71. *Beetles o'er*, Overhangs threateningly.
75. *Toys*, freaks, notions.
83. *Nemean lion* : strangled by Hercules—the first of his twelve
    great " labours."
85. *Lets*, Hinders (*cf.* " let and hindrance ").

SCENE V

Another part of the battlements.

[*The Ghost appears, still followed by Hamlet.*]
Hamlet [*coming to a halt*]. Where wilt thou lead
  me ? speak ; I'll go no further.
Ghost. Mark me.
Hamlet.   I will.
Ghost.   My hour is almost come,
When I to sulphurous and tormenting flames
Must render up myself.
Hamlet.   Alas, poor ghost !
Ghost. Pity me not, but lend thy serious hearing
To what I shall unfold.
Hamlet.   Speak ; I am bound to hear.
Ghost. So art thou to revenge, when thou shalt
  hear.
Hamlet. What ?
Ghost. I am thy father's spirit,
10 Doom'd for a certain term to walk the night,
And for the day confined to fast in fires,
Till the foul crimes done in my days of nature
Are burnt and purged away.   But that I am forbid
To tell the secrets of my prison-house,
I could a tale unfold whose lightest word
Would harrow up thy soul, freeze thy young blood,
Make thy two eyes, like stars, start from their spheres,
Thy knotted and combined locks to part
And each particular hair to stand an end,
20 Like quills upon the fretful porpentine :
But this eternal blazon must not be
To ears of flesh and blood.   List, list, O, list !

---

20. *Porpentine,* Porcupine.
21. *Eternal blazon,* Horrible description, *or* disclosure of the secrets
    of eternity.

If thou didst ever thy dear father love—
    Hamlet. O God !
    Ghost. Revenge his foul and most unnatural
       murder.
    Hamlet. Murder !
    Ghost. Murder most foul, as in the best it is ;
But this most foul, strange and unnatural.
    Hamlet. Haste me to know't, that I, with wings as
      swift
30 As meditation or the thoughts of love,
May sweep to my revenge.
    Ghost.   I find thee apt ;
And duller shouldst thou be than the fat weed
That roots itself in ease on Lethe wharf,
Wouldst thou not stir in this.   Now, Hamlet, hear :
'Tis given out that, sleeping in my orchard,
A serpent stung me ; so the whole ear of Denmark
Is by a forged process of my death
Rankly abused : but know, thou noble youth,
The serpent that did sting thy father's life
40 Now wears his crown.
    Hamlet.   O my prophetic soul !
My uncle !
    Ghost. Ay, that incestuous, that adulterate beast,
With witchcraft of his wit, with traitorous gifts,—
O wicked wit and gifts, that have the power
So to seduce !—won to his shameful lust
The will of my most seeming-virtuous queen :
O Hamlet, what a falling-off was there !
From me, whose love was of that dignity
That it went hand in hand even with the vow
50 I made to her in marriage, and to decline
Upon a wretch whose natural gifts were poor
To those of mine !
But virtue, as it never will be moved,

33. *Lethe,* River of forgetfulness in the Greek underworld of the
    dead. *Wharf,* bank.
35. *Orchard,* Probably " garden."   37. *Process,* Story.

Though lewdness court it in a shape of heaven,
So lust, though to a radiant angel link'd,
Will sate itself in a celestial bed,
And prey on garbage.
But, soft ! methinks I scent the morning air ;
Brief let me be.   Sleeping within my orchard,
60 My custom always of the afternoon,
Upon my secure hour thy uncle stole,
With juice of cursed hebenon in a vial,
And in the porches of my ears did pour
The leperous distilment ; whose effect
Holds such an enmity with blood of man
That swift as quicksilver it courses through
The natural gates and alleys of the body,
And with a sudden vigour it doth posset
And curd, like eager droppings into milk,
70 The thin and wholesome blood ; so did it mine ;
And a most instant tetter bark'd about,
Most lazar-like, with vile and loathsome crust,
All my smooth body.
Thus was I, sleeping, by a brother's hand
Of life, of crown, of queen, at once dispatch'd :
Cut off even in the blossoms of my sin,
Unhousel'd, disappointed, unaneled,
No reckoning made, but sent to my account
With all my imperfections on my head :
80 O, horrible ! O, horrible ! most horrible !
If thou hast nature in thee, bear it not ;
But, howsoever thou pursuest this act,
Taint not thy mind, nor let thy soul contrive
Against thy mother aught : leave her to heaven
And to those thorns that in her bosom lodge,
To prick and sting her.   Fare thee well at once !

---

62. *Hebenon*, Yew (?).   68. *Posset*, Curdle.
69. *Eager*, Acid.   71. *Tetter*, Skin eruption.
72. *Lazar*, Leper.
77. *Unhousel'd*, Not having received the holy sacrament. *Disappointed*, Unprepared, not equipped. *Unaneled*, Unanointed
with extreme unction (Roman Catholic rite).

The glow-worm shows the matin to be near,
90 And 'gins to pale his uneffectual fire :
Adieu, adieu ! Hamlet, remember me.   [*Exit.*]
　Hamlet. O all you host of heaven !   O earth ! what
　　else ?
And shall I couple hell ?   O, fie !   Hold, hold, my
　heart ;
And you, my sinews, grow not instant old,
But bear me stiffly up.   Remember thee !
Ay, thou poor ghost, while memory holds a seat
In this distracted globe.   Remember thee !
Yea, from the table of my memory
I'll wipe away all trivial fond records,
100 All saws of books, all forms, all pressures past,
That youth and observation copied there ;
And thy commandment all alone shall live
Within the book and volume of my brain,
Unmix'd with baser matter : yes, by heaven !
O most pernicious woman !
O villain, villain, smiling, damned villain !
My tables,—meet it is I set it down,
That one may smile, and smile, and be a villain ;
At least I'm sure it may be so in Denmark :
　　　　　　　　　　　　　　　　　[*Writing.*]
110 So, uncle, there you are.   Now to my word ;
It is " Adieu, adieu ! remember me."
I have sworn't.
　Marcellus ⎱ [*within*]. My lord, my lord,—
　Horatio　⎰
　Marcellus [*within*].   Lord Hamlet,
　Horatio [*within*].   Heaven secure him !
　Hamlet. So be it !
　Horatio [*within*]. Hillo, ho, ho, my lord !
　Hamlet. Hillo, ho, ho, boy ! come, bird, come.
　　　　　　[*Enter Horatio and Marcellus.*]
　Marcellus. How is't, my noble lord ?

97. *Distracted globe*, His head.   98. *Table*, Tablet.
　　　100. *Saws*, Maxims.   *Pressures*, Impressions.
38

Horatio.   What news, my lord ?

Hamlet. O, wonderful !

Horatio.   Good my lord, tell it.

Hamlet. No ; you'll reveal it.

120 *Horatio.* Not I, my lord, by heaven.

Marcellus.   Nor I, my lord.

Hamlet. How say you, then ; would heart of man
  once think it ?

But you'll be secret ?

Horatio.   }
Marcellus. }   Ay, by heaven, my lord.

Hamlet. There's ne'er a villain dwelling in all Denmark—

But he's an arrant knave.

Horatio. There needs no ghost, my lord, come from
  the grave

To tell us this.

Hamlet.   Why, right ; you are i' the right ;

And so, without more circumstance at all,

I hold it fit that we shake hands and part :

You, as your business and desire shall point you ;

130 For every man has business and desire,

Such as it is ; and for mine own poor part,

Look you, I'll go pray.

Horatio. These are but wild and whirling words, my
  lord.

Hamlet. I'm sorry they offend you, heartily ;

Yes, 'faith, heartily.

Horatio.   There's no offence, my lord.

Hamlet. Yes, by Saint Patrick, but there is, Horatio,

And much offence too.   Touching this vision here,

It is an honest ghost, that let me tell you :

For your desire to know what is between us,

140 O'ermaster't as you may.   And now, good friends,

As you are friends, scholars and soldiers,

Give me one poor request.

Horatio. What is't, my lord ? we will.

Hamlet. Never make known what you have seen
to-night.

Horatio. }
Marcellus. } My lord, we will not.

Hamlet.   Nay, but swear't.

Horatio.   In faith,
My lord, not I.

Marcellus.   Nor I, my lord, in faith.

Hamlet. Upon my sword.

Marcellus.   We have sworn, my lord, already.

Hamlet. Indeed, upon my sword, indeed.

Ghost [beneath]. Swear.

150 *Hamlet.* Ah, ha, boy ! say'st thou so ? art thou
there, truepenny ?
Come on—you hear this fellow in the cellarage—
Consent to swear.

Horatio.   Propose the oath, my lord.

Hamlet. Never to speak of this that you have seen,
Swear by my sword.

Ghost [beneath]. Swear.

Hamlet. Hic et ubique ? then we'll shift our ground.
Come hither, gentlemen,
And lay your hands again upon my sword :
Never to speak of this that you have heard,
160 Swear by my sword.

Ghost [beneath]. Swear.

Hamlet. Well said, old mole ! canst work i' the
earth so fast ?
A worthy pioner !   Once more remove, good friends.

Horatio. O day and night, but this is wondrous
strange !

Hamlet. And therefore as a stranger give it welcome.
There are more things in heaven and earth, Horatio,

150. *Truepenny*, Honest fellow.
156. *Hic et ubique*, Here and everywhere.
160. *Swear by my sword*, The hilt has the form of a cross.
163. *Pioner*, Digger, miner.

Than are dreamt of in your philosophy.
But come ;
Here, as before, never, so help you mercy,
170 How strange or odd soe'er I bear myself,
As I perchance hereafter shall think meet
To put an antic disposition on,
That you, at such times seeing me, never shall,
With arms encumber'd thus, or this head-shake,
Or by pronouncing of some doubtful phrase,
As " Well, well, we know," or " We could, an if we
     would,"
Or " If we list to speak," or " There be, an if they
     might,"
Or such ambiguous giving out, to note
That you know aught of me : this not to do,
180 So grace and mercy at your most need help you,
     Swear.
     Ghost [*beneath*]. Swear.
     Hamlet. Rest, rest, perturbed spirit ! [*They swear.*]
          So, gentlemen,
With all my love I do commend me to you :
And what so poor a man as Hamlet is
May do, to express his love and friending to you,
God willing, shall not lack.   Let us go in together ;
And still your fingers on your lips, I pray.
The time is out of joint : O cursed spite,
190 That ever I was born to set it right !
Nay, come, let's go together.   [*Exeunt.*]

167. *Your philosophy* : does not mean Horatio's, but simply phi-
     losophy in general. *Cf.* " Your dead body " (page 126,
     line 182).
172. *Antic*, Fantastic, grotesque.

ACT II

SCENE I

A room in Polonius' house.

[*Enter Polonius and Reynaldo.*]
Polonius. Give him this money and these notes,
  Reynaldo.
Reynaldo. I will, my lord.
Polonius. You shall do marvellous wisely, good
  Reynaldo,
Before you visit him, to make inquire
Of his behaviour.
  Reynaldo.   My lord, I did intend it.
Polonius. Marry, well said ; very well said. Look
  you, sir,
Inquire me first what Danskers are in Paris ;
And how, and who, what means, and where they
    keep,
What company, at what expense ; and finding
10 By this encompassment and drift of question
That they do know my son, come you more nearer
Than your particular demands will touch it :
Take you, as 'twere, some distant knowledge of
    him ;
As thus, " I know his father and his friends,
  And in part him : " do you mark this, Reynaldo ?

7. *Danskers*, Danes.

Reynaldo. Ay, very well, my lord.

Polonius. " And in part him ; but " you may say
    " not well :

But, if 't be he I mean, he's very wild ;

Addicted so and so : " and there put on him

20 What forgeries you please ; marry, none so rank

As may dishonour him ; take heed of that ;

But, sir, such wanton, wild and usual slips

As are companions noted and most known

To youth and liberty.

Reynaldo.   As gaming, my lord.

Polonius. Ay, or drinking, fencing, swearing, quar-
    relling ;

But breathe his faults so quaintly

That they may seem the taints of liberty,

The flash and outbreak of a fiery mind,

A savageness in unreclaimed blood,

30 Of general assault.

Reynaldo.   But, my good lord,—

Polonius. Wherefore should you do this ?

Reynaldo.   Ay, my lord,

I would know that.

Polonius.   Marry, sir, here's my drift ;

And, I believe, it is a fetch of wit :

You laying these slight sullies on my son,

As 'twere a thing a little soil'd i' the working,

Mark you,

Your party in converse, him you would sound,

Having ever seen in the prenominate crimes

The youth you breathe of guilty, be assured

40 He closes with you in this consequence ;

" Good sir," or so, or " friend," or " gentleman,"

According to the phrase or the addition

Of man and country.

Reynaldo.   Very good, my lord.

Polonius. And then, sir, does he this—he does—

---

33. *Fetch of wit*, Ingenious device.   42. *Addition*, Title.

what was I about to say ?   By the mass, I was about
to say something : where did I leave ?

   Reynaldo. At " closes in the consequence," at
" friend or so," and " gentleman."

   Polonius. At " closes in the consequence," ay,
       marry ;

50 He closes thus : " I know the gentleman ;
I saw him yesterday, or t' other day,
Or then, or then ; with such, or such ; and, as you say,
There was a' gaming ; there o'ertook in's rouse ;
There falling out at tennis : " or perchance,
" I saw him enter such a house of sale."
See you now ;
Your bait of falsehood takes this carp of truth :
And thus do we of wisdom and of reach,
With windlasses and with assays of bias,
60 By indirections find directions out :
So by my former lecture and advice,
Shall you my son.   You have me, have you not ?

   Reynaldo. My lord, I have.

   Polonius.   God be wi' you ; fare you well.

   Reynaldo. Good my lord !

   Polonius. Observe his inclination in yourself.

   Reynaldo. I shall, my lord.

   Polonius. And let him ply his music.

   Reynaldo.   Well, my lord.

   Polonius. Farewell !   [*Exit Reynaldo.*]

           [*Enter Ophelia.*]

         How now, Ophelia ! what's the matter ?

70   *Ophelia*. O, my lord, my lord, I have been so
       affrighted !

   Polonius. With what, i' the name of God ?

   Ophelia. My lord, as I was sewing in my closet,
Lord Hamlet, with his doublet all unbraced ;

---

53. *O'ertook in's rouse*, Overcome by drink.
59. *Windlasses*, Winding turns. *Assays of bias*, Indirect methods
    (metaphor from the game of bowls).
67. *Ply his music*, Go his own way without interference (?).
72. *Closet*, Private room.   73. *Unbraced*, Unfastened.

No hat upon his head ; his stockings foul'd,
Ungarter'd, and down-gyved to his ankle ;
Pale as his shirt ; his knees knocking each other ;
And with a look so piteous in purport
As if he had been loosed out of hell
To speak of horrors,—he comes before me.

80 *Polonius.* Mad for thy love ?

Ophelia.   My lord, I do not know ;
But truly, I do fear it.

Polonius.   What said he ?

Ophelia. He took me by the wrist and held me
   hard ;
Then goes he to the length of all his arm ;
And, with his other hand thus o'er his brow,
He falls to such perusal of my face
As he would draw it.   Long stay'd he so ;
At last, a little shaking of mine arm
And thrice his head thus waving up and down,
He raised a sigh so piteous and profound
90 As it did seem to shatter all his bulk
And end his being : that done, he lets me go :
And, with his head over his shoulder turn'd,
He seem'd to find his way without his eyes ;
For out o' doors he went without their helps,
And, to the last, bended their light on me.

   Polonius. Come, go with me : I will go seek the
      king.
This is the very ecstasy of love,
Whose violent property fordoes itself
And leads the will to desperate undertakings
100 As oft as any passion under heaven
That does afflict our natures.   I am sorry.
What, have you given him any hard words of late ?

   Ophelia. No, my good lord, but, as you did com-
      mand,
I did repel his letters and denied

---

75. *Down-gyved,* Fallen to his ankles, where they looked like *gyves,*
   fetters.   97. *Ecstasy,* Frenzy.   98. *Fordoes,* Destroys.

His access to me.
 Polonius.   That hath made him mad.
I am sorry that with better heed and judgment
I had not quoted him : I fear'd he did but trifle,
And meant to wreck thee ; but, beshrew my jealousy !
By heaven, it is as proper to our age
110 To cast beyond ourselves in our opinions
As it is common for the younger sort
To lack discretion. Come, go we to the king :
This must be known ; which, being kept close, might move
More grief to hide than hate to utter love.

            [Exeunt.]

SCENE II

A room in the castle.

*[Enter King, Queen, Rosencrantz, Guildenstern, and
Attendants.]*
 King. Welcome, dear Rosencrantz and Guilden-
  stern !
Moreover that we much did long to see you,
The need we have to use you did provoke
Our hasty sending. Something have you heard
Of Hamlet's transformation ; so call it,
Sith nor the exterior nor the inward man
Resembles that it was. What it should be,
More than his father's death, that thus hath put him
So much from the understanding of himself,
10 I cannot dream of : I entreat you both,
That, being of so young days brought up with him,
And sith so neighbour'd to his youth and haviour,
That you vouchsafe your rest here in our court
Some little time : so by your companies

     6. *Sith*, Since.
       46

To draw him on to pleasures, and to gather,
So much as from occasion you may glean,
Whether aught, to us unknown, afflicts him thus,
That, open'd, lies within our remedy.

Queen. Good gentlemen, he hath much talk'd of you ;
20 And sure I am two men there are not living
To whom he more adheres. ˙ If it will please you
To show us so much gentry and good will
As to expend your time with us awhile,
For the supply and profit of our hope,
Your visitation shall receive such thanks
As fits a king's remembrance.

Rosencrantz. Both your majesties
Might, by the sovereign power you have of us,
Put your dread pleasures more into command
Than to entreaty.

Guildenstern. But we both obey,
30 And here give up ourselves, in the full bent
To lay our service freely at your feet,
To be commanded.

King. Thanks, Rosencrantz and gentle Guildenstern.

Queen. Thanks, Guildenstern and gentle Rosencrantz :
And I beseech you instantly to visit
My too much changed son. Go, some of you,
And bring these gentlemen where Hamlet is.

Guildenstern. Heavens make our presence and our practices
Pleasant and helpful to him !

Queen. Ay, amen !

[*Exeunt Rosencrantz, Guildenstern, and some Attendants.*]

[*Enter Polonius.*]

40 *Polonius.* The ambassadors from Norway, my good lord,
Are joyfully return'd.

47

   King. Thou still hast been the father of good news.
   Polonius. Have I, my lord ?   I assure my good
      liege,
I hold my duty, as I hold my soul,
Both to my God and to my gracious king :
And I do think, or else this brain of mine
Hunts not the trail of policy so sure
As it hath used to do, that I have found
The very cause of Hamlet's lunacy.
50   *King.* O, speak of that ; that do I long to hear.
   Polonius. Give first admittance to the ambassadors ;
My news shall be the fruit to that great feast.
   King. Thyself do grace to them, and bring them in.
                           [*Exit Polonius.*]
He tells me, my dear Gertrude, he hath found
The head and source of all your son's distemper.
   Queen. I doubt it is no other but the main ;
His father's death, and our o'erhasty marriage.
   King. Well, we shall sift him.
[*Re-enter Polonius, with Voltimand and Cornelius.*]
                    Welcome, my good friends !
Say, Voltimand, what from our brother Norway ?
60   *Voltimand.* Most fair return of greetings and
      desires.
Upon our first, he sent out to suppress
His nephew's levies ; which to him appear'd
To be a preparation 'gainst the Polack ;
But, better look'd into, he truly found
It was against your highness : whereat grieved,
That so his sickness, age and impotence
Was falsely borne in hand, sends out arrests
On Fortinbras ; which he, in brief, obeys ;
Receives rebuke from Norway, and in fine
70 Makes vow before his uncle never more
To give the assay of arms against your majesty.
Whereon old Norway, overcome with joy,

42. *Still,* always (as usual in Shakespeare).
67. *Falsely borne in hand,* Deluded.

48

Gives him three thousand crowns in annual fee,
And his commission to employ those soldiers,
So levied as before, against the Polack :
With an entreaty, herein further shown,

[Giving a paper.]

That it might please you to give quiet pass
Through your dominions for this enterprise,
On such regards of safety and allowance
80 As therein are set down.
    King.   It likes us well ;
And at our more consider'd time we'll read,
Answer, and think upon this business.
Meantime we thank you for your well-took labour :
Go to your rest ; at night we'll feast together :
Most welcome home !

               [Exeunt Voltimand and Cornelius.]
    Polonius.   This business is well ended.
My liege, and madam, to expostulate
What majesty should be, what duty is,
Why day is day, night night, and time is time,
Were nothing but to waste night, day and time.
90 Therefore, since brevity is the soul of wit,
And tediousness the limbs and outward flourishes,
I will be brief : your noble son is mad :
Mad call I it ; for, to define true madness,
What is't but to be nothing else but mad ?
But let that go.
    Queen.   More matter, with less art.
    Polonius. Madam, I swear I use no art at all.
That he is mad, 'tis true : 'tis true 'tis pity ;
And pity 'tis 'tis true : a foolish figure ;
But farewell it, for I will use no art.
100 Mad let us grant him, then : and now remains
That we find out the cause of this effect,
Or rather say, the cause of this defect,
For this effect defective comes by cause :

---

86. *Expostulate,* Discuss.   90. *Wit,* Intelligence.
  (3,362)

               4

Thus it remains, and the remainder thus.
Perpend.
I have a daughter—have while she is mine—
Who, in her duty and obedience, mark,
Hath given me this : now gather, and surmise.

[Reads.]

" *To the celestial and my soul's idol, the most beautified*
110 *Ophelia,*"—
That's an ill phrase, a vile phrase ; " beautified " is a
vile phrase : but you shall hear.   Thus :   *[Reads.]*
" *In her excellent white bosom, these, etc.*"
    Queen. Came this from Hamlet to her ?
    Polonius. Good madam, stay awhile ; I will be
        faithful.   *[Reads.]*

      " *Doubt thou the stars are fire ;*
        Doubt that the sun doth move ;
        Doubt truth to be a liar ;
        But never doubt I love.

120 " *O dear Ophelia, I am ill at these numbers ; I have*
not art to reckon my groans : but that I love thee best, O
most best, believe it.   Adieu.
    " *Thine evermore, most dear lady, whilst this*
        machine is to him,   HAMLET."

This, in obedience, hath my daughter shown me,
And more above, hath his solicitings,
As they fell out by time, by means and place,
All given to mine ear.
    King.   But how hath she
Received his love ?
    Polonius.   What do you think of me ?
180   *King.* As of a man faithful and honourable.
    Polonius. I would fain prove so.   But what might
        you think,
When I had seen this hot love on the wing—
As I perceived it, I must tell you that,

    105. *Perpend,* Consider.   **124.** *Machine,* Body.

Before my daughter told me—what might you,
Or my dear majesty your queen here, think,
If I had play'd the desk or table-book,
Or given my heart a winking, mute and dumb,
Or look'd upon this love with idle sight ;
What might you think ?   No, I went round to work,
140 And my young mistress thus I did bespeak :
" Lord Hamlet is a prince, out of thy star ;
This must not be : " and then I prescripts gave her,
That she should lock herself from his resort,
Admit no messengers, receive no tokens.
Which done, she took the fruits of my advice ;
And he, repulsed—a short tale to make—
Fell into a sadness, then into a fast,
Thence to a watch, thence into a weakness,
Thence to a lightness, and, by this declension,
150 Into the madness wherein now he raves,
And all we mourn for.
    King.   Do you think 'tis this ?
    Queen. It may be, very likely.
    Polonius. Hath there been such a time—I'd fain
        know that—
That I have positively said " 'Tis so,"
When it proved otherwise ?
    King.   Not that I know.
    Polonius [*pointing to his head and his shoulder*].
        Take this from this, if this be otherwise :
If circumstances lead me, I will find
Where truth is hid, though it were hid indeed
Within the centre.
    King.   How may we try it further ?
160   *Polonius.* You know, sometimes he walks four
        hours together

136. *Play'd . . . table-book*, Kept silence.
156. *This from this :* may mean the chamberlain's staff of office,
    and the hand which holds it ; not his head and his shoulders.
    The stage-direction has been added by the present editor.
159. *Centre*, Of the earth.

Here in the lobby.

 Queen.   So he does indeed.

 Polonius. At such a time I'll loose my daughter to
  him :

Be you and I behind an arras then ;

Mark the encounter : if he love her not

And be not from his reason fall'n thereon,

Let me be no assistant for a state,

But keep a farm and carters.

 King.   We will try it.

 Queen. But, look, where sadly the poor wretch
  comes reading.

 Polonius. Away, I do beseech you, both away :
170 I'll board him presently.

      [*Exeunt King, Queen, and Attendants.*]
      [*Enter Hamlet, reading.*]

 Polonius.   O, give me leave :

How does my good Lord Hamlet ?

 Hamlet. Well, God-a-mercy.

 Polonius. Do you know me, my lord ?

 Hamlet. Excellent well ; you are a fishmonger.

 Polonius. Not I, my lord.

 Hamlet. Then I would you were so honest a man.

 Polonius. Honest, my lord !

 Hamlet. Ay, sir ; to be honest, as this world goes, is
to be one man picked out of ten thousand.

180 *Polonius.* That's very true, my lord.

 Hamlet. For if the sun breed maggots in a dead dog,
being a god kissing carrion,—Have you a daughter ?

 Polonius. I have, my lord.

 Hamlet. Let her not walk i' the sun. Friend, look
to't.

 Polonius [*aside*]. How say you by that ? Still harp-
ing on my daughter : yet he knew me not at first ;
he said I was a fishmonger : he is far gone, far gone :
and truly in my youth I suffered much extremity

190 for love ; very near this. I'll speak to him again.
What do you read, my lord ?

Hamlet. Words, words, words.

Polonius. What is the matter, my lord ?

Hamlet. Between who ?

Polonius. I mean, the matter that you read, my lord.

Hamlet. Slanders, sir : for the satirical rogue says
here that old men have grey beards, that their faces
are wrinkled, their eyes purging thick amber and
plum-tree gum, and that they have a plentiful lack
200 of wit, together with most weak hams : all which, sir,
though I most powerfully and potently believe, yet I
hold it not honesty to have it thus set down, for yourself, sir, should be old as I am, if like a crab you could
go backward.

Polonius [*aside*]. Though this be madness, yet there
is method in't. Will you walk out of the air, my
lord ?

Hamlet. Into my grave.

Polonius. Indeed, that is out o' the air.   [*Aside.*]
210 How pregnant sometimes his replies are ! a happiness
that often madness hits on, which reason and sanity
could not so prosperously be delivered of.   I will leave
him, and suddenly contrive the means of meeting
between him and my daughter.—My honourable lord,
I will most humbly take my leave of you.

Hamlet. You cannot, sir, take from me anything
that I will more willingly part withal : except my
life, except my life, except my life.

Polonius. Fare you well, my lord.

220   *Hamlet.* These tedious old fools !

            [*Enter Rosencrantz and Guildenstern.*]

Polonius. You go to seek the Lord Hamlet ; there
    he is.

Rosencrantz [*to Polonius*]. God save you, sir !

                                    [*Exit Polonius.*]

Guildenstern. My honoured lord !

Rosencrantz. My most dear lord !

Hamlet. My excellent good friends! How dost thou, Guildenstern? Ah, Rosencrantz! Good lads, how do ye both?

Rosencrantz. As the indifferent children of the earth.

230   *Guildenstern.* Happy, in that we are not over-happy;
On fortune's cap we are not the very button.

Hamlet. Nor the soles of her shoe?

Rosencrantz. Neither, my lord.

Hamlet. What's the news?

Rosencrantz. None, my lord, but that the world's grown honest.

Hamlet. Then is doomsday near: but your news is not true. Let me question more in particular: what 240 have you, my good friends, deserved at the hands of fortune, that she sends you to prison hither?

Guildenstern. Prison, my lord!

Hamlet. Denmark's a prison.

Rosencrantz. Then is the world one.

Hamlet. A goodly one; in which there are many confines, wards and dungeons, Denmark being one o' the worst.

Rosencrantz. We think not so, my lord.

Hamlet. Why, then, 'tis none to you; for there is 250 nothing either good or bad, but thinking makes it so; to me it is a prison.

Rosencrantz. Why then, your ambition makes it one; 'tis too narrow for your mind.

Hamlet. O God, I could be bounded in a nutshell and count myself a king of infinite space, were it not that I have bad dreams.

Guildenstern. Which dreams indeed are ambition, for the very substance of the ambitious is merely the shadow of a dream.

260   *Hamlet.* A dream itself is but a shadow.

Rosencrantz. Truly, and I hold ambition of so airy and light a quality that it is but a shadow's shadow.

Hamlet. Then are our beggars bodies, and our monarchs and outstretched heroes the beggars' shadows. Shall we to the court? for, by my fay, I cannot reason.

Rosencrantz. }
Guildenstern. } We'll wait upon you.

Hamlet. No such matter: I will not sort you with the rest of my servants, for, to speak to you like an
270 honest man, I am most dreadfully attended. But, in the beaten way of friendship, what make you at Elsinore?

Rosencrantz. To visit you, my lord; no other occasion.

Hamlet. Beggar that I am, I am even poor in thanks; but I thank you: and sure, dear friends, my thanks are too dear a halfpenny. Were you not sent for? Is it your own inclining? Is it a free visitation? Come, deal justly with me: come, come; nay,
280 speak.

Guildenstern. What should we say, my lord?

Hamlet. Why, anything, but to the purpose. You were sent for; and there is a kind of confession in your looks which your modesties have not craft enough to colour: I know the good king and queen have sent for you?

Rosencrantz. To what end, my lord?

Hamlet. That you must teach me. But let me conjure you, by the rights of our fellowship, by the
290 consonancy of our youth, by the obligation of our ever-preserved love, and by what more dear a better proposer could charge you withal, be even and direct with me, whether you were sent for, or no?

Rosencrantz [*aside to Guildenstern*]. What say you?

Hamlet [*aside*]. Nay, then, I have an eye of you.— If you love me, hold not off.

---

265. *Fay,* Faith.   271. *What make you?* What are you doing?
277. *Dear a halfpenny,* Dear at a halfpenny.
290. *Consonancy,* Harmony, friendship.   292. *Even,* Plain, honest.

Guildenstern. My lord, we were sent for.

Hamlet. I will tell you why ; so shall my anticipation prevent your discovery, and your secrecy to the king and queen moult no feather.   I have of late— but wherefore I know not—lost all my mirth, forgone all custom of exercises ; and indeed it goes so heavily with my disposition that this goodly frame, the earth, seems to me a sterile promontory, this most excellent canopy, the air, look you, this brave o'erhanging firmament, this majestical roof fretted with golden fire, why, it appears no other thing to me than a foul and pestilent congregation of vapours.   What a piece of work is a man ! how noble in reason ! how infinite in faculty ! in form and moving how express and admirable ! in action how like an angel ! in apprehension how like a god ! the beauty of the world ! the paragon of animals !   And yet, to me, what is this quintessence of dust ? man delights not me : no, nor woman neither, though by your smiling you seem to say so.

Rosencrantz. My lord, there was no such stuff in my thoughts.

Hamlet. Why did you laugh then, when I said " man delights not me " ?

Rosencrantz. To think, my lord, if you delight not in man, what lenten entertainment the players shall receive from you : we coted them on the way ; and hither are they coming, to offer you service.

Hamlet. He that plays the king shall be welcome ; his majesty shall have tribute of me ; the adventurous knight shall use his foil and target ; the lover shall not sigh gratis ; the humorous man shall end his part in peace ; the clown shall make those laugh

---

299. *Prevent your discovery,* Anticipate your disclosure.
310. *Express,* well modelled.
314. *Quintessence,* Pure essence or extract.   322. *Lenten,* Meagre.
323. *Coted,* Outstripped, overtook and passed.
328. *Humorous man,* not necessarily "funny man," but actor of capricious, whimsical character parts.   See page 150.

330 whose lungs are tickle o' the sere ; and the lady shall
say her mind freely, or the blank verse shall halt for 't.
What players are they ?

Rosencrantz. Even those you were wont to take
delight in, the tragedians of the city.

Hamlet. How chances it they travel ? their resi-
dence, both in reputation and profit, was better both
ways.

Rosencrantz. I think their inhibition comes by the
means of the late innovation.

340 *Hamlet.* Do they hold the same estimation they did
when I was in the city ? are they so followed ?

Rosencrantz. No, indeed, are they not.

Hamlet. How comes it ? do they grow rusty ?

Rosencrantz. Nay, their endeavour keeps in the
wonted pace : but there is, sir, an aery of children,
little eyases, that cry out on the top of question, and
are most tyrannically clapped for 't : these are now
the fashion, and so berattle the common stages—so
they call them—that many wearing rapiers are afraid
350 of goose-quills and dare scarce come thither.

Hamlet. What, are they children ? who maintains
'em ? how are they escoted ? Will they pursue the
quality no longer than they can sing ? will they not
say afterwards, if they should grow themselves to
common players—as it is most like, if their means are
no better—their writers do them wrong, to make them
exclaim against their own succession ?

Rosencrantz. 'Faith, there has been much to do on

---

330. *Tickle o' the sere,* Easily explode (in laughter). The *sere* was
the catch which held back the hammer of a gun.
338. *Inhibition,* Prohibition.
346. *Eyases,* Young hawks in training.
346. *On the top of question,* In high-pitched voices, above the dis-
pute (?).
349. *Many wearing rapiers,* Adult actors (or perhaps, men of
fashion). *Afraid of goose-quills,* Afraid of satires upon them
which were inserted in the plays acted by the " children " (?).
352. *Escoted,* Maintained, paid for.
353. *Quality,* Profession.

both sides ; and the nation holds it no sin to tarre them
360 to controversy : there was, for a while, no money bid
for argument, unless the poet and the player went to
cuffs in the question.

Hamlet. Is't possible ?

Guildenstern. O, there has been much throwing
about of brains.

Hamlet. Do the boys carry it away ?

Rosencrantz. Ay, that they do, my lord ; Hercules
and his load too.

Hamlet. It is not very strange ; for mine uncle is
370 King of Denmark, and those that would make mows
at him while my father lived, give twenty, forty,
fifty, an hundred ducats a-piece for his picture in
little.   'Sblood, there is something in this more than
natural, if philosophy could find it out.

> [*Flourish of trumpets within.*]

Guildenstern. There are the players.

Hamlet. Gentlemen, you are welcome to Elsinore.
Your hands, come then : the appurtenance of welcome is fashion and ceremony : let me comply with
you in this garb, lest my extent to the players, which,
380 I tell you, must show fairly outward, should more
appear like entertainment than yours.   You are welcome : but my uncle-father and aunt-mother are
deceived.

Guildenstern. In what, my dear lord ?

Hamlet. I am but mad north-north-west : when the
wind is southerly I know a hawk from a handsaw.

> [*Re-enter Polonius.*]

Polonius. Well be with you, gentlemen !

Hamlet. Hark you, Guildenstern ; and you too : at

---

359. *Tarre,* Urge.
367. *Hercules and his load too.* **The sign of the Globe Theatre was**
    Hercules bearing the world on his shoulders.
370. *Mows,* Grimaces.
373. *'Sblood,* By God's blood.
385. *I am but mad, etc.,* I am mad only **on one point.**
386. *Handsaw,* (?) Hernshaw, heron.

each ear a hearer : that great baby you see there is
890 not yet out of his swaddling-clouts.

Rosencrantz. Happily he's the second time come to
them ; for they say an old man is twice a child.

Hamlet. I will prophesy he comes to tell me of the
players ; mark it. You say right, sir : o' Monday
morning ; 'twas so indeed.

Polonius. My lord, I have news to tell you.

Hamlet. My lord, I have news to tell you.   When
Roscius was an actor in Rome,—

Polonius. The actors are come hither, my lord.

400 *Hamlet.* Buz, buz !

Polonius. Upon mine honour,—

Hamlet. Then came each actor on his ass,—

Polonius. The best actors in the world, either for
tragedy, comedy, history, pastoral, pastoral-comical,
historical-pastoral, tragical-historical, tragical-com-
ical-historical-pastoral, scene individable, or poem
unlimited : Seneca cannot be too heavy, nor Plautus
too light.   For the law of writ and the liberty, these
are the only men.

410 *Hamlet.* O Jephthah, judge of Israel, what a treasure hadst thou !

Polonius. What a treasure had he, my lord ?

Hamlet. Why,

" One fair daughter and no more,
      The which he loved passing well."

Polonius [*aside*]. Still on my daughter.

Hamlet. Am I not i' the right, old Jephthah ?

Polonius. If you call me Jephthah, my lord, I have
a daughter that I love passing well.

420 *Hamlet.* Nay, that follows not.

406. *Scene individable*, (?) Play which observes the unity of place.
406. *Poem unlimited*, Not limited by the unities.   See page 151.
407. *Seneca, Plautus*, Latin tragic and comic dramatists, whose
      work influenced Elizabethan drama a good deal.
408. *Writ and the liberty*, (?) Written parts and improvisation.
410. *Jephthah* sacrificed his daughter.   See Judges xi.

Polonius. What follows, then, my lord ?
Hamlet. Why,

　　　" As by lot, God wot."

and then, you know,

　　　" It came to pass, as most like it was,"—

the first row of the pious chanson will show you more ;
for look, where my abridgment comes.

　　　　[Enter four or five Players.]

You are welcome, masters ; welcome, all.　I am glad
to see thee well.　Welcome, good friends.　O, my old
430 friend ! thy face is valanced since I saw thee last :
comest thou to beard me in Denmark ?　What, my
young lady and mistress !　By 'r lady, your ladyship
is nearer to heaven than when I saw you last, by the
altitude of a chopine.　Pray God, your voice, like a
piece of uncurrent gold, be not cracked within the
ring.　Masters, you are all welcome.　We'll e'en to 't
like French falconers, fly at anything we see : we'll
have a speech straight : come, give us a taste of your
quality ; come, a passionate speech.

440 　*First Player.* What speech, my lord ?

　　Hamlet. I heard thee speak me a speech once, but it
was never acted ; or, if it was, not above once ; for
the play, I remember, pleased not the million ; 'twas
caviare to the general : but it was—as I received it,
and others, whose judgments in such matters cried in
the top of mine—an excellent play, well digested in the
scenes, set down with as much modesty as cunning.　I
remember, one said there were no sallets in the lines

---

426. *Pious chanson*, The Elizabethan ballad which Hamlet has been
　　　quoting.　*Row*, Line.
430. *Valanced*, Fringed with a beard.
432. *My young lady* is a boy : a reminder that women's parts were
　　　played by boys until after the Restoration, 1660.
434. *Chopine*, High-heeled shoe.
444. *Caviare to the general* (now proverbial), Too good for popular
　　　taste.　　　　　　　　448. *Sallets*, Salads, spicy flavouring.

to make the matter savoury, nor no matter in the
450 phrase that might indict the author of affectation ;
but called it an honest method, as wholesome as
sweet, and by very much more handsome than fine.
One speech in it I chiefly loved : 'twas Æneas' tale to
Dido ; and thereabout of it especially, where he speaks
of Priam's slaughter : if it live in your memory, begin
at this line : let me see, let me see—

" The rugged Pyrrhus, like the Hyrcanian beast,"—

it is not so :—it begins with Pyrrhus :—

" The rugged Pyrrhus, he whose sable arms,
460 Black as his purpose, did the night resemble
When he lay couched in the ominous horse,
Hath now this dread and black complexion smear'd
With heraldry more dismal ; head to foot
Now is he total gules ; horridly trick'd
With blood of fathers, mothers, daughters, sons,
Baked and impasted with the parching streets,
That lend a tyrannous and damned light
To their lord's murder : roasted in wrath and fire,
And thus o'er-sized with coagulate gore,
470 With eyes like carbuncles, the hellish Pyrrhus
Old grandsire Priam seeks."

So, proceed you.
   Polonius. 'Fore God, my lord, well spoken, with
good accent and good discretion.

   First Player.   " Anon he finds him
Striking too short at Greeks ; his antique sword,
Rebellious to his arm, lies where it falls,
Repugnant to command : unequal match'd,
Pyrrhus at Priam drives ; in rage strikes wide ;
480 But with the whiff and wind of his fell sword
The unnerved father falls.   Then senseless Ilium,

---

457. *Hyrcanian beast*, Tiger.
461. *Ominous horse*, The wooden horse by which the Greeks cap-
     tured Troy.
464. *Gules* (heraldic term), Red. *Trick'd*, Adorned.
466. *Impasted*, Made into a paste.

Seeming to feel this blow, with flaming top
Stoops to his base, and with a hideous crash
Takes prisoner Pyrrhus' ear : for, lo ! his sword,
Which was declining on the milky head
Of reverend Priam, seem'd i' the air to stick :
So, as a painted tyrant, Pyrrhus stood,
And like a neutral to his will and matter,
Did nothing.
490 But, as we often see, against some storm,
A silence in the heavens, the rack stand still,
The bold winds speechless and the orb below
As hush as death, anon the dreadful thunder
Doth rend the region, so, after Pyrrhus' pause,
Aroused vengeance sets him new a-work ;
And never did the Cyclops' hammers fall
On Mars's armour forged for proof eterne
With less remorse than Pyrrhus' bleeding sword
Now falls on Priam.   Out, Fortune !   All you gods,
500 In general synod, take away her power ;
Break all the spokes and fellies from her wheel,
And bowl the round nave down the hill of heaven,
As low as to the fiends ! "

Polonius. This is too long.
Hamlet. It shall to the barber's, with your beard.
Prithee, say on : he's for a jig or a tale of bawdry, or
he sleeps : say on : come to Hecuba.

   First Player. " But who, O, who had seen the mobled
      Queen—"

   Hamlet. " The mobled queen " ?
510 *Polonius.* That's good ; " mobled queen " is good.

   First Player. " Run barefoot up and down, threaten-
      ing the flames
With bissom rheum ; a clout upon that head
Where late the diadem stood, and for a robe,
About her lank and all o'er-teemed loins,
A blanket, in the alarm of fear caught up ;

---

491. *Rack*, Driving storm-clouds.
501. *Fellies*, Sections composing rim.   506. *Bawdry*, Indecency.
508. *Mobled*, muffled.   512. *Bisson rheum,* Blinding tears (?).

Who this had seen, with tongue in venom steep'd,
'Gainst Fortune's state would treason have pronounced:
But if the gods themselves did see her then
When she saw Pyrrhus make malicious sport
520 In mincing with his sword her husband's limbs,
The instant burst of clamour that she made,
Unless things mortal move them not at all,
Would have made milch the burning eyes of heaven,
And passion in the gods."

Polonius. Look, whether he has not turned his
colour and has tears in's eyes. Pray you, no more.

Hamlet. 'Tis well ; I'll have thee speak out the rest
soon. Good my lord, will you see the players well
bestowed ? Do you hear, let them be well used ;
530 for they are the abstract and brief chronicles of the
time : after your death you were better have a bad
epitaph than their ill report while you live.

Polonius. My lord, I will use them according to
their desert.

Hamlet. God's bodykins, man, much better : use
every man after his desert, and who should 'scape
whipping ? Use them after your own honour and
dignity : the less they deserve, the more merit is in
your bounty. Take them in.

540 *Polonius.* Come, sirs.

Hamlet. Follow him, friends : we'll hear a play to-
morrow.

[*Exit Polonius. As the Players are following him
        Hamlet stops the first and draws him aside.*]

Hamlet. Dost thou hear me, old friend ; can you
play the Murder of Gonzago ?

First Player. Ay, my lord.

Hamlet. We'll ha't to-morrow night. You could,
for a need, study a speech of some dozen or sixteen
lines, which I would set down and insert in't, could
you not ?

550 *First Player.* Ay, my lord.

523. *Milch*, here, weep.

Hamlet. Very well. Follow that lord ; and look
you mock him not.

[*Exit the First Player. Hamlet turns to Rosencrantz
    and Guildenstern.*]

Hamlet. My good friends, I'll leave you till night :
you are welcome to Elsinore.

Rosencrantz. Good my lord !

Hamlet. Ay, so, God be wi' ye ;

[*Exeunt Rosencrantz and Guildenstern.*]

Now I am alone.

O, what a rogue and peasant slave am I !
Is it not monstrous that this player here,
But in a fiction, in a dream of passion,
560 Could force his soul so to his own conceit
That from her working all his visage wann'd,
Tears in his eyes, distraction in's aspect,
A broken voice, and his whole function suiting
With forms to his conceit ? and all for nothing !
For Hecuba !
What's Hecuba to him, or he to Hecuba,
That he should weep for her ?   What would he do,
Had he the motive and the cue for passion
That I have ?   He would drown the stage with tears
570 And cleave the general ear with horrid speech,
Make mad the guilty and appal the free,
Confound the ignorant, and amaze indeed
The very faculties of eyes and ears.
Yet I,
A dull and muddy-mettled rascal, peak,
Like John-a-dreams, unpregnant of my cause,
And can say nothing ; no, not for a king,
Upon whose property and most dear life
A damn'd defeat was made.   Am I a coward ?
580 Who calls me villain ? breaks my pate across ?
Plucks off my beard, and blows it in my face ?
Tweaks me by the nose ? gives me the lie i' the throat,

560. *Conceit,* Idea, imagination.   575. *Peak,* Mope about.
576. *Unpregnant of,* Not quickened by.

As deep as to the lungs ? who does me this ?
Ha !
'Swounds, I should take it : for it cannot be
But I am pigeon-liver'd and lack gall
To make oppression bitter, or ere this
I should have fatted all the region kites
With this slave's offal : bloody, bawdy villain !
590 Remorseless, treacherous, lecherous, kindless villain !
O, vengeance !
Why, what an ass am I ! This is most brave,
That I, the son of a dear father murder'd,
Prompted to my revenge by heaven and hell,
Must unpack my heart with words,
And fall a-cursing, like a very drab,
A scullion !
Fie upon 't ! foh ! About, my brain ! I have heard
600 That guilty creatures sitting at a play
Have by the very cunning of the scene
Been struck so to the soul that presently
They have proclaim'd their malefactions ;
For murder, though it have no tongue, will speak
With most miraculous organ. I'll have these players
Play something like the murder of my father
Before mine uncle : I'll observe his looks ;
I'll tent him to the quick : if he but blench,
I know my course. The spirit that I have seen
610 May be the devil : and the devil hath power
To assume a pleasing shape ; yea, and perhaps
Out of my weakness and my melancholy,
As he is very potent with such spirits,
Abuses me to damn me : I'll have grounds
More relative than this : the play's the thing
Wherein I'll catch the conscience of the king.   [*Exit.*]

586. *Pigeon-liver'd*, Gentle, meek. *Gall*, spirit to resent injury.
590. *Kindless*, Unnatural.
602. *Presently*, Instantly (the usual Elizabethan meaning).

ACT III

SCENE I

A room in the castle.

[*Enter King, Queen, Polonius, Ophelia, Rosencrantz,
and Guildenstern.*]

King. And can you, by no drift of circumstance,
Get from him why he puts on this confusion,
Grating so harshly all his days of quiet
With turbulent and dangerous lunacy ?

Rosencrantz. He does confess he feels himself distracted ;
But from what cause he will by no means speak.

Guildenstern. Nor do we find him forward to be
sounded,
But, with a crafty madness, keeps aloof,
When we would bring him on to some confession
10 Of his true state.

Queen.   Did he receive you well ?

Rosencrantz. Most like a gentleman.

Guildenstern. But with much forcing of his disposition.

Rosencrantz. Niggard of question ; but, of our
demands,
Most free in his reply.

Queen.   Did you assay him
To any pastime ?

Rosencrantz. Madam, it so fell out, that certain
players

We o'er-raught on the way : of these we told him ;
And there did seem in him a kind of joy
To hear of it : they are about the court,
20 And, as I think, they have already order
This night to play before him.
    Polonius.   'Tis most true :
And he beseech'd me to entreat your majesties
To hear and see the matter.
    King. With all my heart ; and it doth much con-
        tent me
To hear him so inclined.
Good gentlemen, give him a further edge,
And drive his purpose on to these delights.
    Rosencrantz. We shall, my lord.
               [Exeunt Rosencrantz and Guildenstern.]
    King.   Sweet Gertrude, leave us too ;
For we have closely sent for Hamlet hither,
30 That he, as 'twere by accident, may here
Affront Ophelia :
Her father and myself, lawful espials,
Will so bestow ourselves that, seeing, unseen,
We may of their encounter frankly judge,
And gather by him, as he is behaved,
If 't be the affliction of his love or no
That thus he suffers for.
    Queen.   I shall obey you.
And for your part, Ophelia, I do wish
That your good beauties be the happy cause
40 Of Hamlet's wildness : so shall I hope your virtues
Will bring him to his wonted way again,
To both your honours.
    Ophelia.   Madam, I wish it may.
               [Exit Queen.]
    Polonius. Ophelia, walk you here. Gracious, so
        please you,
We will bestow ourselves. *[To Ophelia, giving her a
        book of prayers.]* Read on this book ;
That show of such an exercise may colour

Your loneliness.   We are oft to blame in this,—
'Tis too much proved—that with devotion's visage
And pious action we do sugar o'er
The devil himself.
    King [*aside*].   O, 'tis too true !
50 How smart a lash that speech doth give my con-
      science !
The harlot's cheek, beautied with plastering art,
Is not more ugly to the thing that helps it
Than is my deed to my most painted word :
O heavy burthen !
    Polonius.   I hear him coming : let's withdraw, my
      lord.
    [*Exeunt King and Polonius.   Ophelia draws aside.*]
      [*Enter Hamlet, deep in troubled thought.*]
    Hamlet.   To be, or not to be : that is the question :
Whether 'tis nobler in the mind to suffer
The slings and arrows of outrageous fortune,
Or to take arms against a sea of troubles,
60 And by opposing end them ?   To die : to sleep ;
No more ; and by a sleep to say we end
The heart-ache and the thousand natural shocks
That flesh is heir to, 'tis a consummation
Devoutly to be wish'd.   To die, to sleep ;
To sleep : perchance to dream : ay, there's the rub ;
For in that sleep of death what dreams may come
When we have shuffled off this mortal coil,
Must give us pause : there's the respect
That makes calamity of so long life ;
70 For who would bear the whips and scorns of time,
The oppressor's wrong, the proud man's contumely,
The pangs of despised love, the law's delay,
The insolence of office and the spurns
That patient merit of the unworthy takes,
When he himself might his quietus make

---

   65. *Rub*, Obstacle (term from bowls).
   67. *Coil*, Trouble, turmoil.
   75. *Quietus* (legal term), Discharge, release from life.

With a bare bodkin ? who would fardels bear,
To grunt and sweat under a weary life,
But that the dread of something after death,
The undiscover'd country from whose bourn
80 No traveller returns, puzzles the will
And makes us rather bear those ills we have
Than fly to others that we know not of ?
Thus conscience does make cowards of us all ;
And thus the native hue of resolution
Is sickled o'er with the pale cast of thought,
And enterprises of great pitch and moment
With this regard their currents turn awry,
And lose the name of action. [*He sees Ophelia*]—
    Soft you now !
The fair Ophelia !—Nymph, in thy orisons
90 Be all my sins remember'd.
    Ophelia.   Good my lord,
How does your honour for this many a day ?
    Hamlet. I humbly thank you ; well, well, well.
    Ophelia. My lord, I have remembrances of yours,
That I have longed long to re-deliver ;
I pray you, now receive them.   [*She offers the gifts.*]
    Hamlet.   No, not I ;
I never gave you aught.
    Ophelia. My honour'd lord, you know right well you
        did ;
And, with them, words of so sweet breath composed
As made the things more rich : their perfume lost,
100 Take these again ; for to the noble mind
Rich gifts wax poor when givers prove unkind.
There, my lord.   [*She offers the gifts.*]
    [*Suddenly Hamlet's manner changes. Perhaps he
        perceives from her confusion, or from a chance
        sound made by one of the spies, that she is acting
        as a decoy to trap him.*]

76. *Bodkin*, Dagger. *Fardels*, Bundles, burdens.
83. *Conscience*, Consciousness, knowledge, inmost thought.
86. *Pitch* (falconry term), Height. *Moment*, Importance.

Hamlet. Ha, ha ! are you honest ?

Ophelia [shrinking]. My lord ?

Hamlet. Are you fair ?

Ophelia. What means your lordship ?

Hamlet. That if you be honest and fair, your honesty should admit no discourse to your beauty.

Ophelia. Could beauty, my lord, have better commerce than with honesty ?

110 *Hamlet.* Ay, truly ; for the power of beauty will sooner transform honesty from what it is than the force of honesty can translate beauty into his likeness : this was sometime a paradox, but now the time gives it proof. I did love you once.

Ophelia. Indeed, my lord, you made me believe so.

Hamlet. You should not have believed me ; for virtue cannot so inoculate our old stock but we shall relish of it : I loved you not.

Ophelia. I was the more deceived.

120 *Hamlet.* Get thee to a nunnery : why wouldst thou be a breeder of sinners ? I am myself indifferent honest ; but yet I could accuse me of such things that it were better my mother had not borne me ; I am very proud, revengeful, ambitious, with more offences at my beck than I have thoughts to put them in, imagination to give them shape, or time to act them in. What should such fellows as I do crawling between earth and heaven ? We are arrant knaves, all ; believe none of us. Go thy ways to a nunnery.

130 Where's your father ?

Ophelia. At home, my lord.

Hamlet. Let the doors be shut upon him, that he may play the fool nowhere but in's own house. Farewell.   [*He turns away.*]

Ophelia. O, help him, you sweet heavens !

Hamlet [rounding upon her]. If thou dost marry, I'll give thee this plague for thy dowry : be thou as

---

117. *Inoculate* (botanical term), Graft on to.
118. *Relish of it,* Keep the evil flavour.

chaste as ice, as pure as snow, thou shalt not escape
calumny. Get thee to a nunnery, go : farewell. Or,
140 if thou wilt needs marry, marry a fool ; for wise men
know well enough what monsters you make of them.
To a nunnery, go, and quickly too. Farewell.

> [*Again he moves away, and again turns wildly upon her.*]

Ophelia. O heavenly powers, restore him !

Hamlet. I have heard of your paintings too, well
enough ; God has given you one face, and you make
yourselves another : you jig, you amble, and you
lisp, and nickname God's creatures, and make your
wantonness your ignorance. Go to, I'll no more on't ;
it hath made me mad. I say, we will have no more
150 marriages : those that are married already, all but
one, shall live ; the rest shall keep as they are. To a
nunnery, go. [*He hurries away.*]

Ophelia. O, what a noble mind is here o'erthrown !
The courtier's, soldier's, scholar's, eye, tongue,
    sword ;
The expectancy and rose of the fair state,
The glass of fashion and the mould of form,
The observed of all observers, quite, quite down !
And I, of ladies most deject and wretched,
That suck'd the honey of his music vows,
160 Now see that noble and most sovereign reason,
Like sweet bells jangled, out of tune and harsh ;
That unmatch'd form and feature of blown youth
Blasted with ecstasy : O, woe is me,
To have seen what I have seen, see what I see !

> [*Re-enter King and Polonius.*]

King. Love ! his affections do not that way tend ;
Nor what he spake, though it lack'd form a little,
Was not like madness. There's something in his
    soul,

---

144. *Your paintings.* Probably the " your " is meant for women
    in general. *Cf.* footnote on page 41.
163. *Ecstasy*, Madness.

O'er which his melancholy sits on brood ;
And I do doubt the hatch and the disclose
170 Will be some danger : which for to prevent,
I have in quick determination
Thus set it down : he shall with speed to England,
For the demand of our neglected tribute :
Haply the seas and countries different
With variable objects shall expel
This something-settled matter in his heart,
Whereon his brains still beating puts him thus
From fashion of himself.   What think you on't ?
    Polonius. It shall do well : but yet do I believe
180 The origin and commencement of his grief
Sprung from neglected love.   How now, Ophelia !
You need not tell us what Lord Hamlet said ;
We heard it all.   My lord, do as you please ;
But, if you hold it fit, after the play
Let his queen mother all alone entreat him
To show his grief : let her be round with him ;
And I'll be placed, so please you, in the ear
Of all their conference.   If she find him not,
To England send him, or confine him where
190 Your wisdom best shall think.
    King.   It shall be so :
Madness in great ones must not unwatch'd go.
                                [Exeunt.]

SCENE II

A hall in the castle.

[Enter Hamlet and the Players.]

    Hamlet. Speak the speech, I pray you, as I pro-
nounced it to you, trippingly on the tongue : but if
you mouth it, as many of your players do, I had as
lief the town-crier spoke my lines.   Nor do not saw

186. *Round,* Plain-spoken, direct.

the air too much with your hand, thus, but use all
gently ; for in the very torrent, tempest, and, as I
may say, the whirlwind of passion, you must acquire
and beget a temperance that may give it smoothness.
O, it offends me to the soul to hear a robustious peri-
10 wig-pated fellow tear a passion to tatters, to very
rags, to split the ears of the groundlings, who for the
most part are capable of nothing but inexplicable
dumb-shows and noise : I would have such a fellow
whipped for o'erdoing Termagant ; it out-herods
Herod : pray you, avoid it.

First Player. I warrant your honour.

Hamlet. Be not too tame neither, but let your own
discretion be your tutor : suit the action to the word,
the word to the action ; with this special observance,
20 that you o'erstep not the modesty of nature : for anything so overdone is from the purpose of playing,
whose end, both at the first and now, was and is, to
hold, as 'twere, the mirror up to nature ; to show
virtue her own feature, scorn her own image, and the
very age and body of the time his form and pressure.
Now this overdone, or come tardy off, though it make
the unskilful laugh, cannot but make the judicious
grieve ; the censure of the which one must in your
allowance o'erweigh a whole theatre of others. O,
30 there be players that I have seen play, and heard
others praise, and that highly, not to speak it pro-
fanely, that, neither having the accent of Christians
nor the gait of Christian, pagan, nor man, have so
strutted and bellowed that I have thought some of
nature's journeymen had made men and not made
them well, they imitated humanity so abominably.

---

11. *Groundlings,* Spectators who paid a penny to stand in the
theatre pit : the most ignorant and noisy part of the Elizabethan audience.

14. *Termagant,* The supposed god of the Mohammedans, who appeared in mediæval mystery plays as a violent, overbearing
personage. *Herod* appeared in the same plays as a blustering
tyrant. 25. *Pressure,* Impress.

35. *Journeymen,* Here, incompetent workmen.

First Player. I hope we have reformed that indifferently with us, sir.

Hamlet. O, reform it altogether. And let those that
40 play your clowns speak no more than is set down
for them ; for there be of them that will themselves
laugh, to set on some quantity of barren spectators to
laugh too ; though, in the meantime, some necessary
question of the play be then to be considered : that's
villainous, and shows a most pitiful ambition in the
fool that uses it.   Go, make you ready.

[Exeunt players.]

[Enter Polonius, Rosencrantz, and Guildenstern.]

How now, my lord ! will the king hear this piece of
work ?

Polonius. And the queen too, and that presently.

50   *Hamlet.* Bid the players make haste.

[Exit Polonius.]

Will you two help to hasten them ?

Rosencrantz. }
Guildenstern. } We will, my lord.

[Exeunt Rosencrantz and Guildenstern.]

Hamlet. What ho ! Horatio !

[Enter Horatio.]

Horatio. Here, sweet lord, at your service.

Hamlet. Horatio, thou art e'en as just a man
As e'er my conversation coped withal.

Horatio. O, my dear lord,—

Hamlet.   Nay, do not think I flatter ;
For what advancement may I hope from thee
That no revenue hast but thy good spirits,
60 To feed and clothe thee ?   Why should the poor be
        flatter'd ?
No, let the candied tongue lick absurd pomp,
And crook the pregnant hinges of the knee
Where thrift may follow fawning.   Dost thou hear ?

38. *Indifferently,* Passably.
56. *As e'er . . . withal,* As ever I talked with.
61. *Candied,* Sugared, flattering.   62. *Pregnant,* Ready, prompt.
63. *Thrift,* Profit.

74

Since my dear soul was mistress of her choice
And could of men distinguish, her election
Hath seal'd thee for herself ; for thou hast been
As one, in suffering all, that suffers nothing,
A man that fortune's buffets and rewards
Hast ta'en with equal thanks : and blest are those
70 Whose blood and judgment are so well commingled,
That they are not a pipe for fortune's finger
To sound what stop she please.   Give me that man
That is not passion's slave, and I will wear him
In my heart's core, ay, in my heart of heart,
As I do thee.—Something too much of this.—
There is a play to-night before the king ;
One scene of it comes near the circumstance
Which I have told thee of my father's death :
I prithee, when thou seest that act afoot,
80 Even with the very comment of thy soul
Observe mine uncle : if his occulted guilt
Do not itself unkennel in one speech,
It is a damned ghost that we have seen,
And my imaginations are as foul
As Vulcan's stithy.   Give him heedful note ;
For I mine eyes will rivet to his face,
And after we will both our judgments join
In censure of his seeming.
     Horatio.   Well, my lord :
If he steal aught the whilst this play is playing,
90 And 'scape detecting, I will pay the theft.
     Hamlet. They are coming to the play ; I must be idle :
Get you a place.
     [*Danish march.   A flourish.   Enter King, Queen,
          Polonius, Ophelia, Rosencrantz, Guildenstern,
          and others.*]
     King. How fares our cousin Hamlet ?
     Hamlet. Excellent, i' faith; of the chameleon's dish:

81. *Occulted,* Hidden.
85. *Vulcan,* Roman god of fire.   *Stithy,* Blacksmith's forge.
94. *Chameleon's dish.*   This lizard was supposed to live on air !

I eat the air, promise-crammed: you cannot feed capons so.

King. I have nothing with this answer, Hamlet; these words are not mine.

Hamlet. No, nor mine now. [*To Polonius.*] My lord, you played once i' the university, you say?

100   *Polonius.* That did I, my lord; and was accounted a good actor.

Hamlet. What did you enact?

Polonius. I did enact Julius Cæsar: I was killed i' the Capitol; Brutus killed me.

Hamlet. It was a brute part of him to kill so capital a calf there. Be the players ready?

Rosencrantz. Ay, my lord; they stay upon your patience.

Queen. Come hither, my dear Hamlet, sit by me.

110   *Hamlet.* No, good mother, here's metal more attractive.   [*He sits at Ophelia's feet.*]

Polonius [*to the king*]. O, ho! do you mark that?

Ophelia. You are merry, my lord.

Hamlet. Who, I?

Ophelia. Ay, my lord.

Hamlet. O God, your only jig-maker. What should a man do but be merry? for, look you, how cheerfully my mother looks, and my father died within these two hours.

120   *Ophelia.* Nay, 'tis twice two months, my lord.

Hamlet. So long? Nay then, let the devil wear black, for I'll have a suit of sables. O heavens! die two months ago, and not forgotten yet? Then there's hope a great man's memory may outlive his life half a year: but, by 'r lady, he must build churches then; or else shall he suffer not thinking on, with the hobby-horse, whose epitaph is "For, O, for, O, the hobby-horse is forgot."

96. *Capons*, Cocks to be fattened for table.
127. *The hobby-horse is forgot*, "The good old days are gone."

Hautboys play.   The dumb-show enters.

[*Enter a King and a Queen very lovingly ; the Queen
embracing him, and he her.   She kneels, and makes
show of protestation unto him.   He takes her up,
and declines his head upon her neck ; lays him
down upon a bank of flowers : she, seeing him
asleep, leaves him.   Anon comes in a fellow, takes
off his crown, kisses it, and pours poison in the
King's ears, and exit.   The Queen returns ; finds
the King dead, and makes passionate action.   The
Poisoner, with some two or three Mutes, comes in
again, seeming to lament with her.   The dead body
is carried away.   The Poisoner wooes the Queen
with gifts : she seems loath and unwilling awhile,
but in the end accepts his love.   Exeunt.*]

Ophelia. What means this, my lord ?
130   *Hamlet.* Marry, this is miching mallecho ; it means
mischief.
Ophelia. Belike this show imports the argument of
the play.

[Enter Prologue.]

Hamlet. We shall know by this fellow : the players
cannot keep counsel ; they'll tell all.
Ophelia. Will he tell us what this show meant ?
Hamlet. Ay, or any show that you'll show him : be
not you ashamed to show, he'll not shame to tell you
what it means.
140   *Ophelia.* You are naught, you are naught : I'll mark
the play.

Prologue. For us, and for our tragedy,
Here stooping to your clemency,
We beg your hearing patiently.   [*Exit.*]

Hamlet. Is this a prologue, or the posy of a ring ?
Ophelia. 'Tis brief, my lord.
Hamlet. As woman's love.

130. *Miching mallecho,* Sneaking mischief.
145. *Posy of a ring,* Motto inscribed inside a ring.

[*Enter two Players, King and Queen.*]

    Player King. Full thirty times hath Phœbus' cart
        gone round
Neptune's salt wash and Tellus' orbed ground,
150 And thirty dozen moons with borrow'd sheen
About the world have times twelve thirties been
Since love our hearts and Hymen did our hands
Unite commutual in most sacred bands.
    Player Queen. So many journeys may the sun and moon
Make us again count o'er ere love be done !
But, woe is me, you are so sick of late,
So far from cheer and from your former state,
That I distrust you. Yet, though I distrust,
Discomfort you, my lord, it nothing must :
160 For women's fear and love holds quantity ;
In neither aught, or in extremity.
Now, what my love is, proof hath made you know ;
And as my love is sized, my fear is so :
Where love is great, the littlest doubts are fear ;
Where little fears grow great, great love grows there.
    Player King. 'Faith, I must leave thee, love, and
        shortly too ;
My operant powers their functions leave to do :
And thou shalt live in this fair world behind,
Honour'd, beloved ; and haply one as kind
170 For husband shalt thou—
    Player Queen.   O, confound the rest !
Such love must needs be treason in my breast :
In second husband let me be accurst !
None wed the second but who kill'd the first.

    Hamlet [*aside*]. Wormwood, wormwood.

    Player Queen. The instances that second marriage
        move
Are base respects of thrift, but none of love.
    Player King. I do believe you think what now you
        speak ;
But what we do determine oft we break.
Purpose is but the slave to memory,
180 Of violent birth, but poor validity :

148. *Thirty times*, *i.e.* Thirty years.
158. *Distrust*, Am anxious about.   175. *Instances*, Motives.
176. *Respects*, Considerations.

Which now, like fruit unripe, sticks on the tree ;
But fall, unshaken, when they mellow be.
Most necessary 'tis that we forget
To pay ourselves what to ourselves is debt :
What to ourselves in passion we propose,
The passion ending, doth the purpose lose.
The violence of either grief or joy
Their own enactures with themselves destroy :
Where joy most revels, grief doth most lament ;
190 Grief joys, joy grieves, on slender accident.
This world is not for aye, nor 'tis not strange
That even our loves should with our fortunes change ;
For 'tis a question left us yet to prove,
Whether love lead fortune, or else fortune love.
The great man down, you mark his favourite flies ;
The poor advanced makes friends of enemies.
And hitherto doth love on fortune tend ;
For who not needs shall never lack a friend,
And who in want a hollow friend doth try,
200 Directly seasons him his enemy.
But, orderly to end where I begun,
Our wills and fates do so contrary run
That our devices still are overthrown ;
Our thoughts are ours, their ends none of our own :
So think thou wilt no second husband wed ;
But die thy thoughts when thy first lord is dead.
    Player Queen. Nor earth to me give food, nor heaven
       light !
Sport and repose lock from me day and night !
To desperation turn my trust and hope !
210 An anchor's cheer in prison be my scope !
Each opposite that blanks the face of joy
Meet what I would have well and it destroy !
Both here and hence pursue me lasting strife,
If, once a widow, ever I be wife !

    Hamlet. If she should break it now !

    Player King. 'Tis deeply sworn.   Sweet, leave me
      here awhile ;

188. *Enactures,* Performances.
210. *An anchor's . . . scope,* Probably, may a hermit's (very frugal)
    fare, and a life in prison, be all that is allowed me.
211. *Opposite that blanks,* Contrary thing that makes pale.

My spirits grow dull, and fain I would beguile
The tedious day with sleep.   [*Sleeps.*]
   Player Queen.   Sleep rock thy brain ;
And never come mischance between us twain !   [*Exit.*]

220 *Hamlet.* Madam, how like you this play ?

   Queen. The lady doth protest too much, methinks.

   Hamlet. O, but she'll keep her word.

   King. Have you heard the argument ? Is there no offence in 't ?

   Hamlet. No, no, they do but jest, poison in jest ; no offence i' the world.

   King. What do you call the play ?

   Hamlet. The Mouse-trap. Marry, how ? Tropically. This play is the image of a murder done in
230 Vienna : Gonzago is the duke's name ; his wife, Baptista : you shall see anon ; 'tis a knavish piece of work : but what o' that ? your majesty and we that have free souls, it touches us not : let the galled jade wince, our withers are unwrung.
[Enter Lucianus.]

   Hamlet. This is one Lucianus, nephew to the king.

   Ophelia. You are as good as a chorus, my lord.

   Hamlet. I could interpret between you and your love, if I could see the puppets dallying.

   Ophelia. You are keen, my lord, you are keen.
240 Still better, and worse.

   Hamlet. So you must take your husbands. Begin, murderer ; . . . leave thy damnable faces, and begin. Come : " the croaking raven doth bellow for revenge."

   Lucianus. Thoughts black, hands apt, drugs fit, and
       time agreeing ;
Confederate season, else no creature seeing ;
Thou mixture rank, of midnight weeds collected,
With Hecate's ban thrice blasted, thrice infected,

228. *Tropically* (first syllable pronounced as " trope "), Figuratively.   233. *Free souls,* Free from guilt.
234. *Jade,* Wretched horse.
247. *Hecate,* A Greek goddess supposed to preside over witchcraft.

Thy natural magic and dire property,
On wholesome life usurp immediately.
> [*Pours the poison into the sleeper's ears.*]

250   *Hamlet.* He poisons him i' the garden for 's estate.
His name 's Gonzago : the story is extant, and writ
in choice Italian : you shall see anon how the murderer gets the love of Gonzago's wife.
> [*With a sudden cry the king springs to his feet.*]

Ophelia. The king rises.
Hamlet. What, frighted with false fire !
Queen. How fares my lord ?
Polonius. Give o'er the play.
King. Give me some light : away !
All. Lights, lights, lights !
> [*Exeunt all but Hamlet and Horatio.*]

260   *Hamlet.* Why, let the stricken deer go weep,
      The hart ungalled play ;
        For some must watch, while some must
        sleep :
      So runs the world away.

Would not this, sir, and a forest of feathers—if the
rest of my fortunes turn Turk with me—with two
Provincial roses on my razed shoes, get me a fellow-
ship in a cry of players, sir ?
Horatio. Half a share.
Hamlet. A whole one, I.

270   For thou dost know, O Damon dear,
        This realm dismantled was
      Of Jove himself ; and now reigns here
        A very, very—pajock.

264. *Feathers*, Much worn on the stage.
265. *Turn Turk*, Turn against me.
266. *Provincial roses*, Ribbon rosettes (? Provençal). *Razed*, Cut, slashed.
266. *Fellowship in a cry*, Partnership in a company.
270. *Damon.* The Greeks Damon and Phintias were famous for their friendship.
273. *Pajock*, Peacock.

Horatio. You might have rhymed.

Hamlet. O good Horatio, I'll take the ghost's word for a thousand pound.   Didst perceive ?

Horatio. Very well, my lord.

Hamlet. Upon the talk of the poisoning ?

Horatio. I did very well note him.

280 *Hamlet.* Ah, ha ! Come, some music ! come, the recorders !

> For if the king like not the comedy,
> Why then, belike, he likes it not, perdy.

Come, some music !
[*Re-enter Rosencrantz and Guildenstern.*]

Guildenstern. Good my lord, vouchsafe me a word with you.

Hamlet. Sir, a whole history.

Guildenstern. The king, sir,—

Hamlet. Ay, sir, what of him ?

290 *Guildenstern.* Is in his retirement marvellous distempered.

Hamlet. With drink, sir ?

Guildenstern. No, my lord, rather with choler.

Hamlet. Your wisdom should show itself more richer to signify this to his doctor : for, for me to put him to his purgation would perhaps plunge him into far more choler.

Guildenstern. Good my lord, put your discourse into some frame and start not so wildly from my affair.

300 *Hamlet.* I am tame, sir : pronounce.

Guildenstern. The queen, your mother, in most great affliction of spirit, hath sent me to you.

Hamlet. You are welcome.

Guildenstern. Nay, good my lord, this courtesy is not of the right breed.   If it shall please you to make

---

281. *Recorder,* Wind instrument like a flute.
283. *Perdy,* from " par Dieu."
291. *Distempered,* Disordered, upset.
293. *Choler,* Bilious disorder, or anger.   299. *Frame,* Order.

me a wholesome answer, I will do your mother's commandment: if not, your pardon and my return shall be the end of my business.

Hamlet. Sir, I cannot.

310 *Guildenstern.* What, my lord?

Hamlet. Make you a wholesome answer; my wit's diseased: but, sir, such answer as I can make, you shall command; or, rather, as you say, my mother: therefore no more, but to the matter: my mother, you say,—

Rosencrantz. Then thus she says; your behaviour hath struck her into amazement and admiration.

Hamlet. O wonderful son, that can so astonish a mother! But is there no sequel at the heels of this 320 mother's admiration? Impart.

Rosencrantz. She desires to speak with you in her closet, ere you go to bed.

Hamlet. We shall obey, were she ten times our mother. Have you any further trade with us?

Rosencrantz. My lord, you once did love me.

Hamlet. So I do still, by these pickers and stealers.

Rosencrantz. Good my lord, what is your cause of distemper? you do, surely, bar the door upon your own liberty, if you deny your griefs to your friend.

330 *Hamlet.* Sir, I lack advancement.

Rosencrantz. How can that be, when you have the voice of the king himself for your succession in Denmark?

Hamlet. Ay, sir, but, "While the grass grows,"— the proverb is something musty.

[*Re-enter Players with recorders.*]

O, the recorders! let me see one.—To withdraw with you:—why do you go about to recover the wind of me, as if you would drive me into a toil?

317. *Admiration,* Astonishment, wonder.
326. *Pickers and stealers,* His hands.
336. *To withdraw with you,* (?) A word with you in private, aside.
337. *Recover the wind* (hunting term), Get to windward. *Toil,* Trap.

Guildenstern. O, my lord, if my duty be too bold,
340 my love is too unmannerly.

Hamlet. I do not well understand that.   [*Offering him the recorder.*] Will you play upon this pipe ?

Guildenstern. My lord, I cannot.

Hamlet. I pray you.

Guildenstern. Believe me, I cannot.

Hamlet. I do beseech you.

Guildenstern. I know no touch of it, my lord.

Hamlet. 'Tis as easy as lying : govern these ventages with your fingers and thumb, give it breath with
350 your mouth, and it will discourse most eloquent
music. Look you, these are the stops.

Guildenstern. But these cannot I command to any
utterance of harmony.; I have not the skill.

Hamlet. Why, look you now, how unworthy a thing
you make of me !   You would play upon me ; you
would seem to know my stops ; you would pluck out
the heart of my mystery ; you would sound me from
my lowest note to the top of my compass : and there
is much music, excellent voice, in this little organ ;
360 yet cannot you make it speak.   'Sblood, do you think
I am easier to be played on than a pipe ?   Call me
what instrument you will, though you can fret me, yet
you cannot play upon me.

[*Enter Polonius.*]

God bless you, sir !

Polonius. My lord, the queen would speak with
you, and presently.

Hamlet. Do you see yonder cloud that's almost in
shape of a camel ?

Polonius. By the mass, and 'tis like a camel, indeed.

370 *Hamlet.* Methinks it is like a weasel.

Polonius. It is backed like a weasel.

---

348. *Ventages, stops,* Holes, and plugs by which they are closed in turn.
362. *Fret,* Annoy, with a pun on the musical term—a ring of gut placed on the finger-board of some instruments to regulate the fingering.

Hamlet. Or like a whale ?

Polonius. Very like a whale.

Hamlet. Then I will come to my mother by and
by. They fool me to the top of my bent. I will
come by and by.

Polonius. I will say so.

Hamlet. By and by is easily said. [*Exit Polonius.*]
Leave me, friends. [*Exeunt all but Hamlet.*]
380 'Tis now the very witching time of night,
When churchyards yawn and hell itself breathes out
Contagion to this world : now could I drink hot blood,
And do such bitter business as the day
Would quake to look on. Soft ! now to my mother.
O heart, lose not thy nature ; let not ever
The soul of Nero enter this firm bosom :
Let me be cruel, not unnatural :
I will speak daggers to her, but use none ;
My tongue and soul in this be hypocrites ;
390 How in my words soever she be shent,
To give them seals never, my soul, consent ! [*Exit.*]

SCENE III

A room in the castle.

[*Enter King, Rosencrantz, and Guildenstern.*]
King. I like him not, nor stands it safe with us
To let his madness range. Therefore prepare you ;
I your commission will forthwith dispatch,
And he to England shall along with you :
The terms of our estate may not endure
Hazard so near us as doth hourly grow
Out of his lunacies.

386. *Nero*, the Roman Emperor, murdered his mother.
390. *Shent*, Rebuked.
391. *Give them seals*, Confirm them with actions.

Guildenstern.   We will ourselves provide :
Most holy and religious fear it is
To keep those many, many bodies safe
10 That live and feed upon your majesty.
   Rosencrantz. The single and peculiar life is bound,
With all the strength and armour of the mind,
To keep itself from noyance ; but much more
That spirit upon whose weal depend and rest
The lives of many.   The cease of majesty
Dies not alone ; but, like a gulf, doth draw
What's near it with it : it is a massy wheel,
Fix'd on the summit of the highest mount,
To whose huge spokes ten thousand lesser things
20 Are mortised and adjoin'd ; which, when it falls,
Each small annexment, petty consequence,
Attends the boisterous ruin.   Never alone
Did the king sigh, but with a general groan.
   King. Arm you, I pray you, to this speedy voyage ;
For we will fetters put upon this fear,
Which now goes too free-footed.
   Rosencrantz.   ⎫
   Guildenstern. ⎬   We will haste us.
          ⎭
        [*Exeunt Rosencrantz and Guildenstern.*]
               [*Enter Polonius.*]
   Polonius. My lord, he's going to his mother's
        closet :
Behind the arras I'll convey myself,
To hear the process ; I'll warrant she'll tax him
        home :
30 And, as you said, and wisely was it said,
'Tis meet that some more audience than a mother,
Since nature makes them partial, should o'erhear
The speech, of vantage.   Fare you well, my liege :
I'll call upon you ere you go to bed,
And tell you what I know.
   King.   Thanks, dear my lord.
                        [*Exit Polonius.*]

14. *Weal*, Welfare.   33. *Of vantage*, From a place of vantage.

O, my offence is rank, it smells to heaven ;
It hath the primal eldest curse upon't,
A brother's murder.   Pray can I not,
Though inclination be as sharp as will :
40 My stronger guilt defeats my strong intent ;
And, like a man to double business bound,
I stand in pause where I shall first begin,
And both neglect.   What if this cursed hand
Were thicker than itself with brother's blood,
Is there not rain enough in the sweet heavens
To wash it white as snow ?   Whereto serves mercy
But to confront the visage of offence ?
And what's in prayer but this two-fold force,
To be forestalled ere we come to fall,
50 Or pardon'd being down ?   Then I'll look up ;
My fault is past.   But, O, what form of prayer
Can serve my turn ?   "Forgive me my foul murder"?
That cannot be ; since I am still possess'd
Of those effects for which I did the murder,
My crown, mine own ambition, and my queen.
May one be pardon'd and retain the offence ?
In the corrupted currents of this world
Offence's gilded hand may shove by justice,
And oft 'tis seen the wicked prize itself
60 Buys out the law ; but 'tis not so above :
There is no shuffling, there the action lies
In his true nature ; and we ourselves compell'd,
Even to the teeth and forehead of our faults,
To give in evidence.   What then ?   what rests ?
Try what repentance can : what can it not ?
Yet what can it when one can not repent ?
O wretched state !   O bosom black as death !
O limed soul, that, struggling to be free,
Art more engaged !   Help, angels !   Make assay !
70 Bow, stubborn knees ; and, heart with strings of steel,
Be soft as sinews of the new-born babe !

---

37. *Eldest curse*, The curse of Cain.   68 *Limed*, Trapped.

All may be well.   [*Retires and kneels.*]
                 [*Enter Hamlet.*]
  Hamlet. Now might I do it pat, now he is praying ;
And now I'll do't. [*He draws his rapier and then*
    pauses.] And so he goes to heaven ;
And so am I revenged.   That would be scann'd :
A villain kills my father ; and for that,
I, his sole son, do this same villain send
To heaven.
O, this is hire and salary, not revenge.
80 He took my father grossly, full of bread ;
With all his crimes broad blown, as flush as May ;
And how his audit stands who knows save heaven ?
But in our circumstance and course of thought,
'Tis heavy with him : and am I then revenged,
To take him in the purging of his soul,
When he is fit and season'd for his passage ?
No !
Up, sword ; and know thou a more horrid hent :
When he is drunk asleep, or in his rage,
90 At gaming, swearing, or about some act
That has no relish of salvation in't ;
Then trip him, that his heels may kick at heaven,
And that his soul may be as damn'd and black
As hell, whereto it goes.   My mother stays :
This physic but prolongs thy sickly days.   [*Exit.*]
    King [*rising*]. My words fly up, my thoughts re-
    main below :
Words without thoughts never to heaven go.   [*Exit.*]

    80. *Grossly,* Unshriven.
    88. *Hent,* Grasp, or purpose, or opportunity (?).

SCENE IV

The Queen's room.

[*Enter the Queen and Polonius.*]

Polonius. He will come straight. Look you lay
   home to him :
Tell him his pranks have been too broad to bear with,
And that your grace hath screen'd and stood between
Much heat and him.   I'll sconce me even here.
Pray you, be round with him.
   Hamlet [*within*]. Mother, mother, mother !
   Queen.   I'll warrant you,
Fear me not : withdraw, I hear him coming.
                    [*Polonius hides behind the arras.*]
                    [*Enter Hamlet.*]
   Hamlet. Now, mother, what's the matter ?
   Queen. Hamlet, thou hast thy father much offended.
10   *Hamlet.* Mother, you have my father much offended.
   Queen. Come, come, you answer with an idle
      tongue.
   Hamlet. Go, go, you question with a wicked tongue.
   Queen. Why, how now, Hamlet !
   Hamlet.   What's the matter now ?
   Queen. Have you forgot me ?
   Hamlet.   No, by the rood, not so :
You are the queen, your husband's brother's wife ;
And—would it were not so !—you are my mother.
   Queen. Nay, then, I'll set those to you that can
      speak.   [*She turns to go out.*]
   Hamlet. Come, come, and sit you down ; you shall
      not budge ;
You go not till I set you up a glass
20 Where you may see the inmost part of you.

---

4. *Sconce*, Entrench, hide.   14. *Rood*, Cross.

Queen. What wilt thou do ? thou wilt not murder
    me ?
Help, help, ho !
    Polonius [*behind*]. What, ho ! help, help, help !
    Hamlet [*drawing*]. How now ! a rat ? Dead, for a
    ducat, dead !
                [*He makes a pass through the arras.*]
    Polonius [*behind*]. O, I am slain !   [*Falls and dies.*]
    Queen. O me, what hast thou done ?
    Hamlet.   Nay, I know not :
Is it the king ?
    Queen. O, what a rash and bloody deed is this !
    Hamlet. A bloody deed ! almost as bad, good
    mother,
As kill a king, and marry with his brother.
30   *Queen.* As kill a king !
    Hamlet.   Ay, lady, 'twas my word.
       [*He lifts up the arras and discovers Polonius.*]
Thou wretched, rash, intruding fool, farewell !
I took thee for thy better : take thy fortune ;
Thou find'st to be too busy is some danger.
                  [*He turns to his mother.*]
Leave wringing of your hands : peace ! sit you down,
And let me wring your heart ; for so I shall,
If it be made of penetrable stuff,
If damned custom have not brass'd it so
That it be proof and bulwark against sense.
    Queen. What have I done, that thou darest wag thy
    tongue
40 In noise so rude against me ?
    Hamlet.   Such an act
That blurs the grace and blush of modesty,
Calls virtue hypocrite, takes off the rose
From the fair forehead of an innocent love
And sets a blister there, makes marriage-vows
As false as dicers' oaths : O, such a deed

---

23. *Ducat,* Gold or silver coin, value here uncertain.

As from the body of contraction plucks
The very soul, and sweet religion makes
A rhapsody of words : heaven's face doth glow ;
Yea, this solidity and compound mass,
50 With tristful visage, as against the doom,
Is thought-sick at the act.
  Queen.   Ay me, what act,
That roars so loud, and thunders in the index ?
  Hamlet. Look here, upon this picture, and on **this,**
The counterfeit presentment of two brothers.
See, what a grace was seated on this brow ;
Hyperion's curls ; the front of Jove himself ;
An eye like Mars, to threaten and command ;
A station like the herald Mercury
New-lighted on a heaven-kissing hill ;
60 A combination and a form indeed,
Where every god did seem to set his seal,
To give the world assurance of a man :
This was your husband. Look you now, what **follows:**
Here is your husband ; like a mildew'd ear,
Blasting his wholesome brother. Have you eyes ?
Could you on this fair mountain leave to feed,
And batten on this moor ? Ha ! have you eyes ?
You cannot call it love ; for at your age
The hey-day in the blood is tame, it's humble,
70 And waits upon the judgment : and what judg-
   ment
Would step from this to this ? Sense, sure, you have,
Else could you not have motion ; but sure, that
   sense
Is apoplex'd ; for madness would not err,
Nor sense to ecstasy was ne'er so thrall'd
But it reserved some quantity of choice,

46. *Contraction*, Here, marriage-contract.
49. *This solidity*, The earth.
50. *Tristful*, Sorrowful.
52. *Index* (at the beginning of a book), Beginning.
53. *This picture . . . this*, Either miniatures, or portraits on the
  wall.   67. *Batten*, Grow fat.

To serve in such a difference.   What devil was 't
That thus hath cozen'd you at hoodman-blind ?
Eyes without feeling, feeling without sight,
Ears without hands or eyes, smelling sans all,
80 Or but a sickly part of one true sense
Could not so mope.
O shame ! where is thy blush ?   Rebellious hell,
If thou canst mutine in a matron's bones,
To flaming youth let virtue be as wax,
And melt in her own fire : proclaim no shame
When the compulsive ardour gives the charge,
Since frost itself as actively doth burn
And reason pandars will.
    Queen.   O Hamlet, speak no more :
Thou turn'st mine eyes into my very soul ;
90 And there I see such black and grained spots
As will not leave their tinct.
    Hamlet.   Nay, but to live
Stew'd in corruption, honeying and making love
Over the nasty sty,—
    Queen.   O, speak to me no more ;
These words, like daggers, enter in mine ears ;
No more, sweet Hamlet !
    Hamlet.   A murderer and a villain :
A slave that is not twentieth part the tithe
Of your precedent lord ; a vice of kings ;
A cutpurse of the empire and the rule,
100 That from a shelf the precious diadem stole,
And put it in his pocket !
    Queen.   No more !
    Hamlet. A king of shreds and patches,—
                [The Ghost appears.]
Save me, and hover o'er me with your wings,

77. *Cozen'd*, Cheated.   *Hoodman-blind*, Blind-man's buff.
79. *Sans*, Without.   81. *Mope*, Be bewildered, act aimlessly.
88. *Pandars*, Ministers to the gratification of.
90. *Grained*, Indelibly stained.
91. *Leave their tinct*, Change their colour.
98. *Vice*, The fool in mediæval plays.

You heavenly guards ! What would your gracious
    figure ?
   Queen. Alas, he's mad !
   Hamlet. Do you not come your tardy son to
    chide,
That, lapsed in time and passion, lets go by
The important acting of your dread command ?
O, say !
110   *Ghost.* Do not forget : this visitation
Is but to whet thy almost blunted purpose.
But, look, amazement on thy mother sits :
O, step between her and her fighting soul :
Conceit in weakest bodies strongest works :
Speak to her, Hamlet.
    Hamlet.   How is it with you, lady ?
   Queen. Alas, how is't with you,
That you do bend your eye on vacancy
And with the incorporal air do hold discourse ?
Forth at your eyes your spirits wildly peep ;
120 And, as the sleeping soldiers in the alarm,
Your bedded hair, like life in excrements,
Start up, and stand an end. O gentle son,
Upon the heat and flame of thy distemper
Sprinkle cool patience. Whereon do you look ?
   Hamlet. On him, on him ! Look you, how pale he
    glares !
His form and cause conjoin'd, preaching to stones,
Would make them capable. Do not look upon me ;
Lest with this piteous action you convert
My stern effects : then what I have to do
130 Will want true colour ; tears perchance for blood.
   Queen. To whom do you speak this ?
   Hamlet.   Do you see nothing there ?
   Queen. Nothing at all ; yet all that is I see.
   Hamlet. Nor did you nothing hear ?
   Queen.   No, nothing but ourselves.

---

118. *Incorporal,* Immaterial.   121. *Excrements,* Outgrowths.
        127. *Capable,* susceptible.

Hamlet. Why, look you there ! look, how it steals
    away !
My father, in his habit as he lived !
Look, where he goes, even now, out at the portal !
                            [Exit Ghost.]

Queen. This is the very coinage of your brain :
This bodiless creation ecstasy
Is very cunning in.

    Hamlet.   Ecstasy !

140 My pulse, as yours, doth temperately keep time,
And makes as healthful music : it is not madness
That I have utter'd : bring me to the test,
And I the matter will re-word ; which madness
Would gambol from.   Mother, for love of grace,
Lay not that flattering unction to your soul,
That not your trespass, but my madness speaks :
It will but skin and film the ulcerous place,
Whiles rank corruption, mining all within,
Infects unseen.   Confess yourself to heaven ;
150 Repent what's past ; avoid what is to come ;
And do not spread the compost on the weeds,
To make them ranker.   Forgive me this my virtue ;
For in the fatness of these pursy times
Virtue itself of vice must pardon beg,
Yea, curb and woo for leave to do him good.

    Queen. O Hamlet, thou hast cleft my heart in
    twain.

    Hamlet. O, throw away the worser part of it,
And live the purer with the other half.
Assume a virtue, if you have it not.
160 That monster, custom, who all sense doth eat,
Of habits devil, is angel yet in this,
That to the use of actions fair and good
He likewise gives a frock or livery,
That aptly is put on.   Refrain,

---

135. *Habit*, Dress.   151. *Compost*, Manure.
153. *Pursy*, Short-winded (from fatness).
155. *Curb*, Kneel, bend.   164. *Aptly*, Easily.

And that shall lend a kind of easiness
To the next abstinence ; the next more easy ;
For use almost can change the stamp of nature,
And either [master] the devil, or throw him out
With wondrous potency.   Once more, good night :
170 And when you are desirous to be bless'd,
I'll blessing beg of you.   For this same lord,

> [*Pointing to Polonius.*]

I do repent : but heaven hath pleased it so,
To punish me with this and this with me,
That I must be their scourge and minister.
I will bestow him, and will answer well
The death I gave him.   So, again, good night.
I must be cruel, only to be kind :
Thus bad begins and worse remains behind.
One word more, good lady.
    Queen.   What shall I do ?
180   *Hamlet.* Not this, by no means, that I bid you do :
Let the bloat king tempt you again ;
Pinch wanton on your cheek ; call you his mouse ;
And let him, for a pair of reechy kisses,
Or paddling in your neck with his damn'd fingers,
Make you to ravel all this matter out,
That I essentially am not in madness,
But mad in craft.   'Twere good you let him know ;
For who, that's but a queen, fair, sober, wise,
Would from a paddock, from a bat, a gib,
190 Such dear concernings hide ? who would do so ?
No, in despite of sense and secrecy,
Unpeg the basket on the house's top,
Let the birds fly, and, like the famous ape,
To try conclusions, in the basket creep,
And break your own neck down.
    Queen. Be thou assured, if words be made of breath,
And breath of life, I have no life to breathe

---

189. *Paddock*, Toad. *Gib*, Tom-cat.
193. *Famous ape*, Reference untraced.
194. *Conclusions*, Experiments.

What thou hast said to me.

    Hamlet. I must to England ; you know that ?

    Queen.   Alack,

200 I had forgot : 'tis so concluded on.

    Hamlet. There's letters seal'd : and my two school-
        fellows,

Whom I will trust as I will adders fang'd,

They bear the mandate ; they must sweep my way,

And marshal me to knavery.   Let it work ;

For 'tis the sport to have the enginer

Hoist with his own petar : and 't shall go hard

But I will delve one yard below their mines,

And blow them at the moon : O, 'tis most sweet,

When in one line two crafts directly meet.

210 This man shall set me packing :

I'll lug the guts into the neighbour room.

Mother, good night.   Indeed this counsellor

Is now most still, most secret and most grave,

Who was in life a foolish prating knave.

Come, sir, to draw toward an end with you.

Good night, mother.

                  *[Exeunt separately ; Hamlet dragging out
                       Polonius.]*

205-6. *The enginer hoist with his own petar,* The engineer blown up
by his own bomb.

ACT IV

SCENE I

A room in the castle.

[*Enter King, Queen, Rosencrantz, and Guildenstern.*]
    King. There's matter in these sighs, these profound heaves :
You must translate : 'tis fit we understand them.
Where is your son ?
    Queen. Bestow this place on us a little while.
                [*Exeunt Rosencrantz and Guildenstern.*]
Ah, mine own lord, what have I seen to-night !
    King. What, Gertrude ?   How does Hamlet ?
    Queen. Mad as the sea and wind, when both contend
Which is the mightier : in his lawless fit,
Behind the arras hearing something stir,
10 Whips out his rapier, cries, " A rat, a rat ! "
And, in this brainish apprehension, kills
The unseen good old man.
    King.   O heavy deed !
It had been so with us, had we been there :
His liberty is full of threats to all ;
To you yourself, to us, to every one.
Alas, how shall this bloody deed be answer'd ?
It will be laid to us, whose providence

---

11. *Brainish,* Headstrong, passionate.

Should have kept short, restrain'd and out of haunt,
This mad young man : but so much was our love,
20 We would not understand what was most fit ;
But, like the owner of a foul disease,
To keep it from divulging, let it feed
Even on the pith of life.   Where is he gone ?
   Queen. To draw apart the body he hath kill'd :
O'er whom his very madness, like some ore
Among a mineral of metals base,
Shows itself pure ; he weeps for what is done.
   King. O Gertrude, come away !
The sun no sooner shall the mountains touch,
30 But we will ship him hence : and this vile deed
We must, with all our majesty and skill,
Both countenance and excuse.   Ho, Guildenstern !
       [Re-enter Rosencrantz and Guildenstern.]
Friends both, go join you with some further aid :
Hamlet in madness hath Polonius slain,
And from his mother's closet hath he dragg'd him :
Go seek him out ; speak fair, and bring the body
Into the chapel.   I pray you, haste in this.
       [Exeunt Rosencrantz and Guildenstern.]
Come, Gertrude, we'll call up our wisest friends ;
And let them know, both what we mean to do,
40 And what's untimely done : [so, haply, slander]
Whose whisper o'er the world's diameter,
As level as the cannon to his blank,
Transports his poison'd shot, may miss our name,
And hit the woundless air.   O, come away !
My soul is full of discord and dismay.   *[Exeunt.]*

    25. *Ore,* (?) Gold.   26. *Mineral,* Mine.
        42. *Blank,* white centre of the target.

SCENE II

Another room in the castle.

[Enter Hamlet.]

Hamlet. Safely stowed.

Rosencrantz } *[within].* Hamlet! Lord Hamlet!
Guildenstern

Hamlet. But soft, what noise? who calls on
      Hamlet?
O, here they come.

[Enter Rosencrantz and Guildenstern.]

Rosencrantz. What have you done, my lord, with
      the dead body?

Hamlet. Compounded it with dust, whereto 'tis kin.

Rosencrantz. Tell us where 'tis, that we may take it
      thence
And bear it to the chapel.

Hamlet. Do not believe it.

10 *Rosencrantz.* Believe what?

Hamlet. That I can keep your counsel and not mine
own. Besides, to be demanded of a sponge! what
replication should be made by the son of a king?

Rosencrantz. Take you me for a sponge, my lord?

Hamlet. Ay, sir, that soaks up the king's countenance, his rewards, his authorities. But such officers
do the king best service in the end: he keeps them,
like an ape, in the corner of his jaw; first mouthed, to
be last swallowed: when he needs what you have
20 gleaned, it is but squeezing you, and, sponge, you
shall be dry again.

Rosencrantz. I understand you not, my lord.

Hamlet. I am glad of it: a knavish speech sleeps
in a foolish ear.

---

12. *Demanded of,* Questioned by.   13. *Replication,* Reply.
              15. *Countenance,* Favour.

Rosencrantz. My lord, you must tell us where the body is, and go with us to the king.

Hamlet. The body is with the king, but the king is not with the body. The king is a thing—

Guildenstern. A thing, my lord !

30 *Hamlet.* Of nothing : bring me to him. Hide, fox, and all after. *[Exeunt.]*

SCENE III

Another room in the castle.

[Enter the King.]
King. I have sent to seek him, and to find the body.
How dangerous is it that this man goes loose !
Yet must not we put the strong law on him :
He's loved of the distracted multitude,
Who like not in their judgment, but their eyes :
And where 'tis so, the offender's scourge is weigh'd,
But never the offence. To bear all smooth and even,
This sudden sending him away must seem
Deliberate pause : diseases desperate grown
10 By desperate appliance are relieved,
Or not at all.
[Enter Rosencrantz.]
How now ! what hath befall'n ?
Rosencrantz. Where the dead body is bestow'd, my lord,
We cannot get from him.
King. But where is he ?
Rosencrantz. Without, my lord ; guarded, to know your pleasure.
King. Bring him before us.
Rosencrantz. Ho, Guildenstern ! bring in my lord.

27. *The body, etc.,* Deliberate nonsense.
30. *Hide fox, etc.,* Probably a signal-cry in hide-and-seek.
9. *Deliberate pause,* The result of deliberation.

[*Enter Hamlet, Guildenstern, and Attendants.*]

King. Now, Hamlet, where's Polonius ?

Hamlet. At supper.

King. At supper ! where ?

20 *Hamlet.* Not where he eats, but where he is eaten : a certain convocation of politic worms are e'en at him. Your worm is your only emperor for diet : we fat all creatures else to fat us, and we fat ourselves for maggots : your fat king and your lean beggar is but variable service, two dishes, but to one table : that's the end.

King. Alas, alas !

Hamlet. A man may fish with the worm that hath eat of a king, and eat of the fish that hath fed of that 30 worm.

King. What dost thou mean by this ?

Hamlet. Nothing but to show you how a king may go a progress through the guts of a beggar.

King. Where is Polonius ?

Hamlet. In heaven ; send thither to see : if your messenger find him not there, seek him i' the other place yourself. But indeed, if you find him not within this month, you shall nose him as you go up the stairs into the lobby.

40 *King* [*to Attendants*]. Go seek him there.

Hamlet. He will stay till you come.

[*Exeunt Attendants.*]

King. Hamlet, this deed, for thine especial safety,—
Which we do tender, as we dearly grieve
For that which thou hast done,—must send thee hence
With fiery quickness : therefore prepare thyself ;
The bark is ready, and the wind at help,
The associates tend, and everything is bent
For England.

Hamlet. For England !

King. Ay, Hamlet.

21. *Politic worms*, Fussy (?) or bred in a politician (?).
33. *Progress*, Royal journey in state. 43. *Tender*, Care for.

Hamlet.   Good.

King. So is it, if thou knew'st our purposes.

50 *Hamlet.* I see a cherub that sees them. But, come ;
for England ! Farewell, dear mother.

King. Thy loving father, Hamlet.

Hamlet. My mother : father and mother is man
and wife ; man and wife is one flesh ; and so, my
mother. Come, for England !   [*Exit.*]

King. Follow him at foot ; tempt him with speed
         aboard ;
Delay it not ; I'll have him hence to-night :
Away ! for everything is seal'd and done
That else leans on the affair : pray you, make haste.
                [*Exeunt Rosencrantz and Guildenstern.*]

60 And, England, if my love thou hold'st at aught—
As my great power thereof may give thee sense,
Since yet thy cicatrice looks raw and red
After the Danish sword, and thy free awe
Pays homage to us—thou mayst not coldly set
Our sovereign process ; which imports at full,
By letters congruing to that effect,
The present death of Hamlet. Do it, England ;
For like the hectic in my blood he rages,
And thou must cure me. Till I know 'tis done
70 Howe'er my haps, my joys were ne'er begun.
                                          [*Exit.*]

SCENE IV

A plain in Denmark.

[*Enter Fortinbras, a Captain, and Soldiers,
                marching.*]

Fortinbras. Go, captain, from me greet the Danish
         king ;
Tell him that, by his license, Fortinbras

62. *Cicatrice,* Scar.   64. *Coldly set,* Ignore.
67. *Present,* Immediate.   68. *Hectic,* Fever.

Craves the conveyance of a promised march
Over his kingdom. You know the rendezvous.
If that his majesty would aught with us,
We shall express our duty in his eye ;
And let him know so.

Captain. I will do't, my lord.

Fortinbras. Go softly on.

[Exeunt Fortinbras and Soldiers.]
[Enter Hamlet, Rosencrantz, Guildenstern, and others.]

Hamlet. Good sir, whose powers are these ?

10 *Captain.* They are of Norway, sir.

Hamlet. How purposed, sir, I pray you ?

Captain. Against some part of Poland.

Hamlet. Who commands them, sir ?

Captain. The nephew to old Norway, Fortinbras.

Hamlet. Goes it against the main of Poland, sir,
Or for some frontier ?

Captain. Truly to speak, and with no addition,
We go to gain a little patch of ground
That hath in it no profit but the name.
20 To pay five ducats, five, I would not farm it ;
Nor will it yield to Norway or the Pole
A ranker rate, should it be sold in fee.

Hamlet. Why, then the Polack never will defend it.

Captain. Yes, it is already garrison'd.

Hamlet. Two thousand souls and twenty thousand ducats
Will not debate the question of this straw :
This is the imposthume of much wealth and peace,
That inward breaks, and shows no cause without
Why the man dies. I humbly thank you, sir.

30 *Captain.* God be wi' you, sir. *[Exit.]*

Rosencrantz. Will't please you go, my lord ?

Hamlet. I'll be with you straight. Go a little before. *[Exeunt all except Hamlet.]*

6. *In his eye,* In his presence (court term). 8. *Softly,* Slowly.
22. *Ranker,* Richer. 27. *Imposthume,* Abscess.

How all occasions do inform against me,
And spur my dull revenge !   What is a man,
If his chief good and market of his time
Be but to sleep and feed ? a beast, no more.
Sure, he that made us with such large discourse,
Looking before and after, gave us not
That capability and god-like reason
To fust in us unused.   Now whether it be
40 Bestial oblivion, or some craven scruple
Of thinking too precisely on the event,
A thought which, quarter'd, hath but one part wisdom
And ever three parts coward, I do not know
Why yet I live to say " This thing's to do ; "
Sith I have cause and will and strength and means
To do't.   Examples gross as earth exhort me :
Witness this army of such mass and charge
Led by a delicate and tender prince,
Whose spirit with divine ambition puff'd
50 Makes mouths at the invisible event,
Exposing what is mortal and unsure
To all that fortune, death, and danger dare,
Even for an egg-shell.   Rightly to be great
Is not to stir without great argument,
But greatly to find quarrel in a straw
When honour 's at the stake.   How stand I then,
That have a father kill'd, a mother stain'd,
Excitements of my reason and my blood,
And let all sleep ? while, to my shame, I see
60 The imminent death of twenty thousand men,
That, for a fantasy and trick of fame,
Go to their graves like beds, fight for a plot
Whereon the numbers cannot try the cause,
Which is not tomb enough and continent
To hide the slain ?   O, from this time forth,
My thoughts be bloody, or be nothing worth !   [*Exit.*]

36. *Discourse*, Reasoning power.   39. *Fust*, Grow mouldy.
41. *Event*, Consequences.   50. *Makes mouths*, Mocks.
54. *Argument*, Reason.   64. *Continent*, Container, receptacle.

SCENE V

Elsinore.   A room in the castle.

[*Enter Queen, Horatio, and a Gentleman.*]
Queen. I will not speak with her.
Gentleman. She is importunate, indeed distract :
Her mood will needs be pitied.
Queen.   What would she have ?
Gentleman. She speaks much of her father ; says
     she hears
There's tricks i' the world ; and hems, and beats her
     heart ;
Spurns enviously at straws ; speaks things in doubt,
That carry but half sense : her speech is nothing,
Yet the unshaped use of it doth move
The hearers to collection ; they aim at it,
10 And botch the words up fit to their own thoughts ;
Which, as her winks, and nods, and gestures yield
     them,
Indeed would make one think there might be thought,
Though nothing sure, yet much unhappily.
Horatio. 'Twere good she were spoken with ; for
     she may strew
Dangerous conjectures in ill-breeding minds.
Queen. Let her come in.   [*Exit Horatio.*]
To my sick soul, as sin's true nature is,
Each toy seems prologue to some great amiss :
So full of artless jealousy is guilt,
20 It spills itself in fearing to be spilt.
          [*Re-enter Horatio, with Ophelia.*]
Ophelia. Where is the beauteous majesty of Den-
     mark ?
Queen. How now, Ophelia !

9. *Collection,* Inference, interpretation.   18. *Toy,* Trifle.
          19. *Jealousy,* Suspicion.

Ophelia [*sings*]. *How should I your true love know*
    From another one ?
   By his cockle hat and staff,
    And his sandal shoon.

Queen. Alas, sweet lady, what imports this song ?
Ophelia. Say you ? nay, pray you, mark.
 [*Sings.*] *He is dead and gone, lady,*
    He is dead and gone ;
   At his head a grass-green turf,
    At his heels a stone.

Queen. Nay, but, Ophelia,—
Ophelia. Pray you, mark.
 [*Sings.*] *White his shroud as the mountain snow,—*
    [*Enter King.*]
Queen. Alas, look here, my lord.
Ophelia [*sings*]. *Larded with sweet flowers ;*
    Which bewept to the grave did go
    With true-love showers.

King. How do you, pretty lady ?
Ophelia. Well, God 'ild you ! They say the owl was
a baker's daughter. Lord, we know what we are,
but know not what we may be. God be at your
table !

King. Conceit upon her father.
Ophelia. Pray you, let's have no words of this ; but
when they ask you what it means, say you this :
 [*Sings.*] *To-morrow is Saint Valentine's day,*
    All in the morning betime,
    And I a maid at your window,
    To be your Valentine.

King. Pretty Ophelia !
Ophelia. Indeed, la, without an oath, I'll make an
end on't :

25. *Cockle hat,* Hat with a scallop shell stuck in it, to show that the
  wearer had been on pilgrimage to the shrine of St. James of
  Compostella, in Spain.   37. *Larded,* Decorated.
41. *'ild,* Yield, reward.   45. *Conceit,* Thinking, brooding.

[*Sings.*] *By Gis and by Saint Charity,*
    Alack, and fie for shame!

King. How long hath she been thus?

Ophelia. I hope all will be well. We must be
patient: but I cannot choose but weep, to think they
60 should lay him i' the cold ground. My brother shall
know of it: and so I thank you for your good counsel.
Come, my coach! Good night, ladies; good night,
sweet ladies; good night, good night. [*Exit.*]

 King. Follow her close; give her good watch, I
  pray you. [*Exit Horatio.*]
O, this is the poison of deep grief; it springs
All from her father's death. O Gertrude, Gertrude,
When sorrows come, they come not single spies,
But in battalions. First, her father slain:
Next, your son gone; and he most violent author
70 Of his own just remove: the people muddied,
Thick and unwholesome in their thoughts and
  whispers,
For good Polonius' death; and we have done but
  greenly,
In hugger-mugger to inter him: poor Ophelia
Divided from herself and her fair judgment,
Without the which we are pictures, or mere beasts:
Last, and as much containing as all these,
Her brother is in secret come from France;
Feeds on his wonder, keeps himself in clouds,
And wants not buzzers to infect his ear
80 With pestilent speeches of his father's death;
Wherein necessity, of matter beggar'd,
Will nothing stick our person to arraign
In ear and ear. O my dear Gertrude, this,
Like to a murdering-piece, in many places
Gives me superfluous death.

---

55. *Gis*, Jesus.   72. *Greenly*, Foolishly.
73. *In hugger-mugger*, Secretly.
84. *Murdering-piece*, Cannon firing many small shot.

[*There is a sudden tumult outside ; shouts, and the
    clash of arms, and hammering blows upon a door.*]
Queen.   Alack, what noise is this ?
King. Where are my Switzers ?   Let them guard
    the door.
            [*Enter another Gentleman.*]
What is the matter ?
    Gentleman.   Save yourself, my lord :
The ocean, overpeering of his list,
Eats not the flats with more impetuous haste
90 Than young Laertes, in a riotous head,
O'erbears your officers.   The rabble call him lord ;
And, as the world were now but to begin,
Antiquity forgot, custom not known,
The ratifiers and props of every word,
They cry " Choose we : Laertes shall be king : "
Caps, hands, and tongues, applaud it to the clouds :
" Laertes shall be king, Laertes king ! "
    Queen. How cheerfully on the false trail they cry !
O, this is counter, you false Danish dogs !
                    [*There is a splintering crash.*]
100   *King.* The doors are broke.
            [*Enter Laertes, sword in hand, with a crowd of
                        Danes at his heels.*]
    Laertes. Where is this king ?   Sirs, stand you all
        without.
    Danes. No, let's come in.
    Laertes.   I pray you, give me leave.
    Danes. We will, we will.
                    [*They retire without the door.*]
    Laertes. I thank you : keep the door.   [*He advances
        threateningly on Claudius.*]   O thou vile king,
Give me my father !
    Queen [*interposing*]. Calmly, good Laertes.
    King.   What is the cause, Laertes,

88. *Overpeering of his list,* Overflowing its bounds.
90. *Head,* Hostile advance.
99. *Counter,* Following the scent backwards (hunting term).

That thy rebellion looks so giant-like ?
Let him go, Gertrude ; do not fear our person :
There's such divinity doth hedge a king,
That treason can but peep to what it would,
110 Acts little of his will.   Tell me, Laertes,
Why art thou thus incensed ?   Let him go, Gertrude.
Speak, man.

    Laertes. Where is my father ?
    King.   Dead.
    Queen [*again interposing*].   But not by him.
    King. Let him demand his fill.
    Laertes. How came he dead ?   I'll not be juggled
       with :

To hell, allegiance ! vows, to the blackest devil !
Conscience and grace, to the profoundest pit !
I dare damnation.   To this point I stand,
That both the worlds I give to negligence,
Let come what comes ; only I'll be revenged
120 Most thoroughly for my father.
    King.   Who shall stay you ?
    Laertes. My will, not all the world :
And for my means, I'll husband them so well,
They shall go far with little.
    King.   Good Laertes,
If you desire to know the certainty
Of your dear father's death, is't writ in your revenge,
That, swoopstake, you will draw both friend and foe,
Winner and loser ?
    Laertes. None but his enemies.
    King.   Will you know them then ?
    Laertes. To his good friends thus wide I'll ope my
       arms ;
130 And like the kind life-rendering pelican,
Repast them with my blood.

---

126. *Swoopstake,* Indiscriminately (taking revenge on your friends
    as well as your foes).
130. *Pelican,* Popularly supposed to feed its young with its own
    blood.

    King.   Why, now you speak
Like a good child and a true gentleman.
That I am guiltless of your father's death,
And am most sensibly in grief for it,
It shall as level to your judgment pierce
As day does to your eye.
    Danes [*within*].   Let her come in.
    Laertes. How now ! what noise is that ?
             [*Re-enter Ophelia.*]
O heat, dry up my brains ! tears seven times salt,
Burn out the sense and virtue of mine eye !
140 By heaven, thy madness shall be paid with weight,
Till our scale turn the beam.   O rose of May !
Dear maid, kind sister, sweet Ophelia !
O heavens ! is't possible, a young maid's wits
Should be as mortal as an old man's life ?
Nature is fine in love, and where 'tis fine,
It sends some precious instance of itself
After the thing it loves.
    Ophelia [*sings*]. *They bore him barefaced on the bier ;*
        Hey non nonny, nonny, hey nonny ;
150   *And in his grave rain'd many a tear :—*

Fare you well, my dove !
    Laertes. Hadst thou thy wits, and didst persuade
        revenge,
It could not move thus.
    Ophelia [*sings*]. *You must sing a-down a-down,*
        An you call him a-down-a.

O, how the wheel becomes it !   It is the false steward,
that stole his master's daughter.
    Laertes. This nothing's more than matter.
    Ophelia [*to Laertes*]. There's rosemary, that 's for

---

134. *Sensibly,* Feelingly.
156. *How the wheel becomes it,* What a good accompaniment to the
    song, (the sound of ?) the spinning-wheel makes (?).
156. *False steward,* Reference unknown.
158. *Matter,* Sense.

160 remembrance ; pray, love, remember : and there is
pansies, that's for thoughts.

Laertes. A document in madness, thoughts and remembrance fitted.

Ophelia [*to the King*]. There's fennel for you, and
columbines : [*to the Queen*] there's rue for you ; and
here's some for me : we may call it herb-grace o'
Sundays : O, you must wear your rue with a difference. There's a daisy : I would give you some
violets, but they withered all when my father died :
170 they say he made a good end,—

[*Sings.*] *For bonny sweet Robin is all my joy.*

Laertes. Thought and affliction, passion, hell itself,
She turns to favour and to prettiness.

Ophelia [*sings*]. *And will he not come again ?*
And will he not come again ?
No, no, he is dead :
Go to thy death-bed :
He never will come again.

His beard was as white as snow,
180 *All flaxen was his poll :*
He is gone, he is gone,
And we cast away moan :
God ha' mercy on his soul !

And of all Christian souls, I pray God. God be
wi' ye.   [*Exit.*]

Laertes. Do you see this, O God ?

King. Laertes, I must commune with your grief,
Or you deny me right.   Go but apart,
Make choice of whom your wisest friends you will,
190 And they shall hear and judge 'twixt you and me :
If by direct or by collateral hand
They find us touch'd, we will our kingdom give,
Our crown, our life, and all that we call ours,
To you in satisfaction ; but if not,

191. *Collateral*, Here, indirect.

III

Be you content to lend your patience to us,
And we shall jointly labour with your soul
To give it due content.
 Laertes.   Let this be so ;
His means of death, his obscure funeral—
No trophy, sword, nor hatchment o'er his bones,
200 No noble rite nor formal ostentation—
Cry to be heard, as 'twere from heaven to earth,
That I must call't in question.
 King.   So you shall ;
And where the offence is let the great axe fall.
I pray you, go with me.   *[Exeunt.]*

SCENE VI

Another room in the castle.

[Enter Horatio and a Servant.]
 Horatio. What are they that would speak with me ?
 Servant. Sailors, sir : they say they have letters for
you.
 Horatio. Let them come in.   *[Exit Servant.]*
I do not know from what part of the world
I should be greeted, if not from lord Hamlet.
    [Enter Sailors.]
 First Sailor. God bless you, sir.
 Horatio. Let him bless thee too.
 First Sailor. He shall, sir, an't please him. There's
10 a letter for you, sir : it comes from the ambassador
that was bound for England ; if your name be
Horatio, as I am let to know it is.

 Horatio [reads]. " *Horatio, when thou shalt have over-
looked this, give these fellows some means to the king:
they have letters for him. Ere we were two days old at*

199. *Hatchment,* Tablet bearing the coat of arms.

sea, *a pirate of very warlike appointment gave us chase.
Finding ourselves too slow of sail, we put on a compelled
valour, and in the grapple I boarded them : on the instant they got clear of our ship ; so I alone became their*
20*prisoner. They have dealt with me like thieves of
mercy : but they knew what they did ; I am to do a
good turn for them. Let the king have the letters I have
sent ; and repair thou to me with as much speed as thou
wouldst fly death. I have words to speak in thine ear
will make thee dumb ; yet are they much too light for the
bore of the matter. These good fellows will bring thee
where I am. Rosencrantz and Guildenstern hold their
course for England : of them I have much to tell thee.
Farewell.*

30   " *He that thou knowest thine,* HAMLET."

Come, I will make you way for these your letters ;
And do't the speedier, that you may direct me
To him from whom you brought them.   [*Exeunt.*]

SCENE VII

Another room in the castle.

[*Enter King and Laertes.*]
King. Now must your conscience my acquittance
        seal,
And you must put me in your heart for friend,
Sith you have heard, and with a knowing ear,
That he which hath your noble father slain
Pursued my life.
    Laertes.   It well appears : but tell me
Why you proceeded not against these feats,
So crimeful and so capital in nature,

---

26. *Bore,* Calibre, capacity.

As by your safety, wisdom, all things else,
You mainly were stirr'd up.

   King.   O, for two special reasons ;
10 Which may to you, perhaps, seem much unsinew'd,
But yet to me they are strong. The queen his mother
Lives almost by his looks ; and for myself—
My virtue or my plague, be it either which—
She's so conjunctive to my life and soul,
That, as the star moves not but in his sphere,
I could not but by her. The other motive,
Why to a public count I might not go,
Is the great love the general gender bear him ;
Who, dipping all his faults in their affection,
20 Would, like the spring that turneth wood to stone,
Convert his gyves to graces ; so that my arrows,
Too slightly timber'd for so loud a wind,
Would have reverted to my bow again,
And not where I had aim'd them.

   Laertes. And so have I a noble father lost ;
A sister driven into desperate terms,
Whose worth, if praises may go back again,
Stood challenger on mount of all the age
For her perfections : but my revenge will come.

30   *King.* Break not your sleeps for that : you must not think
That we are made of stuff so flat and dull
That we can let our beard be shook with danger
And think it pastime.   You shortly shall hear more :
I loved your father, and we love ourself ;
And that, I hope, will teach you to imagine—

               [*Enter a Messenger.*]

How now ! what news ?

   Messenger.   Letters, my lord, from Hamlet :

---

18. *General gender*, Common people.
20. *Spring*, Of water ; *e.g.* at King's Newnham, Warwickshire.
21. *Gyves*, Fetters.
27. *Go back again*, To the days of Ophelia's sanity.

This to your majesty ; this to the queen.

    King. From Hamlet ! who brought them ?

    Messenger. Sailors, my lord, they say ; I saw them
      not ;

40 They were given me by Claudio ; he received them
Of him that brought them.

    King.   Laertes, you shall hear them.
Leave us.   [*Exit Messenger.*]

[*Reads.*] " *High and mighty, You shall know I am set
naked on your kingdom. To-morrow shall I beg leave
to see your kingly eyes : when I shall, first asking your
pardon thereunto, recount the occasion of my sudden and
more strange return.*

                          " HAMLET."

What should this mean ? Are all the rest come back ?
50 Or is it some abuse, and no such thing ?

    Laertes. Know you the hand ?

    King.   'Tis Hamlet's character. " Naked ! "
And in a postscript here, he says " alone."
Can you advise me ?

    Laertes. I'm lost in it, my lord. But let him come ;
It warms the very sickness in my heart,
That I shall live and tell him to his teeth,
" Thus didest thou."

    King.   If it be so, Laertes—
As how should it be so ? how otherwise ?—
Will you be ruled by me ?

    Laertes.   Ay, my lord ;
60 So you will not o'errule me to a peace.

    King. To thine own peace. If he be now return'd,
As checking at his voyage, and that he means
No more to undertake it, I will work him
To an exploit, now ripe in my device,
Under the which he shall not choose but fall :
And for his death no wind of blame shall breathe,

---

    50. *Abuse,* Deception.   **51.** *Naked,* Destitute.

But even his mother shall uncharge the practice
And call it accident.

   Laertes.   My lord, I will be ruled ;
The rather, if you could devise it so
70 That I might be the organ.

   King.   It falls right.
You have been talk'd of since your travel much,
And that in Hamlet's hearing, for a quality
Wherein, they say, you shine : your sum of parts
Did not together pluck such envy from him
As did that one, and that, in my regard,
Of the unworthiest siege.

   Laertes.   What part is that, my lord ?

   King. A very riband in the cap of youth,
Yet needful too ; for youth no less becomes
80 The light and careless livery that it wears
Than settled age his sables and his weeds,
Importing health and graveness.   Two months since,
Here was a gentleman of Normandy :—
I've seen myself, and served against, the French,
And they can well on horseback : but this gallant
Had witchcraft in 't ; he grew unto his seat ;
And to such wondrous doing brought his horse,
As he had been incorpsed and demi-natured
With the brave beast : so far he topp'd my thought,
That I, in forgery of shapes and tricks,
90 Come short of what he did.

   Laertes.   A Norman was't ?

   King. A Norman.

   Laertes. Upon my life, Lamond.

   King.   The very same.

   Laertes. I know him well : he is the brooch indeed
And gem of all the nation.

   King. He made confession of you,

---

76. *Siege* (literally, seat), Rank, value.
81. *Weeds,* Garments (*cf.* widow's weeds).
82. *Health,* Prosperity, well-being.
89. *Forgery,* Invention.   93. *Brooch,* Ornament.

And gave you such a masterly report
For art and exercise in your defence
And for your rapier most especial,
That he cried out, 'twould be a sight indeed,
If one could match you : the scrimers of their nation,
100 He swore, had neither motion, guard, nor eye,
If you opposed them.   Sir, this report of his
Did Hamlet so envenom with his envy
That he could nothing do but wish and beg
Your sudden coming o'er, to play with him.
Now, out of this,—

    Laertes.   What out of this, my lord ?

    King. Laertes, was your father dear to you ?
Or are you like the painting of a sorrow,
A face without a heart ?

    Laertes.   Why ask you this ?

    King. Not that I think you did not love your father ;
110 But that I know love is begun by time ;
And that I see, in passages of proof,
Time qualifies the spark and fire of it.
There lives within the very flame of love
A kind of wick or snuff that will abate it ;
And nothing is at a like goodness still ;
For goodness, growing to a plurisy,
Dies in his own too much : that we would do,
We should do when we would ; for this " would "
      changes
And hath abatements and delays as many
120 As there are tongues, are hands, are accidents ;
And then this " should " is like a spendthrift sigh,
That hurts by easing. But, to the quick o' the
      ulcer :—
Hamlet comes back : what would you undertake,
To show yourself your father's son in deed
More than in words ?

---

99. *Scrimers*, Fencers.   116. *Plurisy*, Excess.
121. *Spendthrift sigh*, Because every sigh was supposed to shorten life.

Laertes.   To cut his throat i' the church.

King. No place, indeed, should murder sanctuarize ;
Revenge should have no bounds.   But, good Laertes,
Will you do this, keep close within your chamber.
Hamlet return'd shall know you are come home :
130 We'll put on those shall praise your excellence
And set a double varnish on the fame
The Frenchman gave you, bring you in fine together
And wager on your heads : he, being remiss,
Most generous and free from all contriving,
Will not peruse the foils ; so that, with ease,
Or with a little shuffling, you may choose
A sword unbated, and in a pass of practice
Requite him for your father.

Laertes.   I will do't :
And, for that purpose, I'll anoint my sword.
140 I bought an unction of a mountebank,
So mortal that, but dip a knife in it,
Where it draws blood no cataplasm so rare,
Collected from all simples that have virtue
Under the moon, can save the thing from death
That is but scratch'd withal : I'll touch my point
With this contagion, that, if I gall him slightly,
It may be death.

King.   Let's further think of this ;
Weigh what convenience both of time and means
May fit us to our shape : if this should fail,
150 And that our drift look through our bad perform-
          ance,
'Twere better not assay'd : therefore this project
Should have a back or second, that might hold,
If this should blast in proof.   Soft ! let me see :
We'll make a solemn wager on your cunnings ;
I ha't :

137. *Unbated,* Not blunted; not protected by the usual button.
137. *Pass of practice,* Treacherous thrust.
140. *Mountebank,* Quack doctor.   142. *Cataplasm,* Plaster.
143. *Simples,* Herbs.   150. *Drift,* Purpose.

When in your motion you are hot and dry—
As make your bouts more violent to that end—
And that he calls for drink, I'll have prepared him
A chalice for the nonce, whereon but sipping,
160 If he by chance escape your venom'd stuck,
Our purpose may hold there.

[Enter Queen.]

                  How now, sweet queen !

Queen. One woe doth tread upon another's heel,
So fast they follow ; your sister's drown'd, Laertes.

Laertes. Drown'd ! O, where ?

Queen. There is a willow grows aslant a brook,
That shows his hoar leaves in the glassy stream ;
There with fantastic garlands did she come
Of crow-flowers, nettles, daisies, and long purples.
There, on the pendent boughs her coronet weeds
170 Clambering to hang, an envious sliver broke ;
When down her weedy trophies and herself
Fell in the weeping brook. Her clothes spread
    wide ;
And, mermaid-like, awhile they bore her up :
Which time she chanted snatches of old tunes,
As one incapable of her own distress,
Or like a creature native and indued
Unto that element : but long it could not be
Till that her garments, heavy with their drink,
Pull'd the poor wretch from her melodious lay
180 To muddy death.

Laertes.   Alas, then, she is drown'd ?

Queen. Drown'd, drown'd.

Laertes. Too much of water hast thou, poor Ophelia,
And therefore I forbid my tears : but yet
It is our trick ; nature her custom holds,
Let shame say what it will : when these are gone,
The woman will be out. Adieu, my lord :

166. *Hoar leaves,* Silver grey on the under side.
170. *Sliver,* Branch.
175. *Incapable of,* Unable to realize, understand.

119

I have a speech of fire, that fain would blaze,
But that this folly douts it.   [*Exit.*]
 King.   Let's follow, Gertrude :
How much I had to do to calm his rage !
190 Now fear I this will give it start again ;
Therefore let's follow.   [*Exeunt.*]

   188. *Folly,* His tears.   *Douts,* Extinguishes.

ACT V

SCENE I

A churchyard.

[*Enter two Clowns, with spades, etc.*]

First Clown. Is she to be buried in Christian burial that wilfully seeks her own salvation ?

Second Clown. I tell thee she is : and therefore make her grave straight : the crowner hath sat on her, and finds it Christian burial.

First Clown. How can that be, unless she drowned herself in her own defence ?

Second Clown. Why, 'tis found so.

First Clown. It must be *se offendendo* ; it cannot be else. For here lies the point : if I drown myself wittingly, it argues an act : and an act hath three branches ; it is, to act, to do, and to perform : argal, she drowned herself wittingly.

Second Clown. Nay, but hear you, goodman delver,—

First Clown. Give me leave [*throwing down his spade*]. Here lies the water ; good ; [*moving a short distance away*] here stands the man ; good : if the man go to this water, and drown himself, it is, will he, nill he, he goes,—mark you that ; but if the water come to him and drown him, he drowns not himself :

4. *Crowner*, Coroner.
9. *Se offendendo*, should be *se defendendo*, in self-defence.
12. *Argal* (ergo), Therefore.

argal, he that is not guilty of his own death shortens not his own life.

Second Clown. But is this law ?

First Clown. Ay, marry, is't ; crowner's quest law.

Second Clown. Will you ha' the truth on't ? If this had not been a gentlewoman, she should have been buried out o' Christian burial.

30 *First Clown.* Why, there thou say'st : and the more pity that great folk should have countenance in this world to drown or hang themselves, more than their even Christian. Come, my spade. There is no ancient gentlemen but gardeners, ditchers, and grave-makers : they hold up Adam's profession.

Second Clown. Was he a gentleman ?

First Clown. A' was the first that ever bore arms.

Second Clown. Why, he had none.

First Clown. What, art a heathen ? How dost 40 thou understand the Scripture ? The Scripture says " Adam digged " : could he dig without arms ? I'll put another question to thee : if thou answerest me not to the purpose, confess thyself—

Second Clown. Go to.

First Clown. What is he that builds stronger than either the mason, the shipwright, or the carpenter ?

Second Clown. The gallows-maker ; for that frame outlives a thousand tenants.

First Clown. I like thy wit well, in good faith : the 50 gallows does well ; but how does it well ? it does well to those that do ill : now thou dost ill to say the gallows is built stronger than the church : argal, the gallows may do well to thee. To't again, come.

Second Clown. " Who builds stronger than a mason, a shipwright, or a carpenter ? "

First Clown. Ay, tell me that, and unyoke.

Second Clown. Marry, now I can tell.

31. *Countenance,* Favour, permission.　　33. *Even,* Fellow.
56. *Unyoke,* Finish work, have done.

First Clown. To't.

Second Clown. Mass, I cannot tell.

[*Enter Hamlet and Horatio, at a distance.*]

60 *First Clown.* Cudgel thy brains no more about it, for your dull ass will not mend his pace with beating ; and, when you are asked this question next, say " a grave-maker " : the houses that he makes last till doomsday. Go, get thee to Yaughan : fetch me a stoup of liquor. [*Exit Second Clown.*]

[*The First Clown begins to dig a grave, singing as he works.*]

> *In youth, when I did love, did love,*
> *Methought it was very sweet,*
> *To contract, O, the time, for, ah, my behove,*
> *O, methought, there was nothing meet.*

70 *Hamlet.* Has this fellow no feeling of his business, that he sings at grave-making ?

Horatio. Custom hath made it in him a property of easiness.

Hamlet. 'Tis e'en so : the hand of little employment hath the daintier sense.

First Clown [*sings*].

> *But age, with his stealing steps,*
> *Hath claw'd me in his clutch,*
> *And hath shipped me intil the land,*
> *As if I had never been such.*

[*He throws up a skull.*]

80 *Hamlet.* That skull had a tongue in it, and could sing once : how the knave jowls it to the ground, as if it were Cain's jaw-bone, that did the first murder ! It might be the pate of a politician, which this ass now o'er-reaches ; one that would circumvent God, might it not ?

65. *Stoup*, Half-gallon measure. 68. *Behove*, Benefit, advantage.
82. *Cain's jaw-bone.* Refers to the legend that Cain slew Abel with the jaw-bone of an ass. 83. *Politician*, Cunning schemer.

Horatio. It might, my lord.

Hamlet. Or of a courtier ; which could say " Good morrow, sweet lord ! How dost thou, good lord ? " This might be my lord such-a-one, that praised my
90 lord such-a-one's horse, when he meant to beg it ; might it not ?

Horatio. Ay, my lord.

Hamlet. Why, e'en so : and now my Lady Worm's ; chapless, and knocked about the mazzard with a sexton's spade : here's fine revolution, an we had the trick to see't. Did these bones cost no more the breeding, but to play at loggats with 'em ? mine ache to think on't.

First Clown [*sings*].

>   *A pick-axe, and a spade, a spade,*
100 >   *For and a shrouding sheet :*
>   *O, a pit of clay for to be made*
>   *For such a guest is meet.*

> [*He throws up another skull.*]

Hamlet. There's another : why may not that be the skull of a lawyer ? Where be his quiddities now, his quillets, his cases, his tenures, and his tricks ? why does he suffer this rude knave now to knock him about the sconce with a dirty shovel, and will not tell him of his action of battery ? Hum ! This fellow might be in's time a great buyer of land, with
110 his statutes, his recognizances, his fines, his double vouchers, his recoveries : is this the fine of his fines, and the recovery of his recoveries, to have his fine pate full of fine dirt ? will his vouchers vouch him no more of his purchases, and double ones too, than the length and breadth of a pair of indentures ? The very conveyances of his lands will hardly lie in this box ; and must the inheritor himself have no more, ha ?

94. *Chapless*, Without a jaw. *Mazzard*, Head.
97. *Loggats*, Game in which thick sticks were thrown like quoits.
107. *Sconce*, Head.

Horatio. Not a jot more, my lord.

120 *Hamlet.* Is not parchment made of sheep-skins ?

Horatio. Ay, my lord, and of calf-skins too.

Hamlet. They are sheep and calves which seek out assurance in that. I will speak to this fellow. Whose grave's this, sirrah ?

First Clown. Mine, sir.

> [*Sings.*] *O, a pit of clay for to be made*
> *For such a guest is meet.*

Hamlet. I think it be thine indeed ; for thou liest in't.

130 *First Clown.* You lie out on't, sir, and therefore it is not yours : for my part, I do not lie in't, and yet it is mine.

Hamlet. Thou dost lie in't, to be in't and say it is thine : 'tis for the dead, not for the quick ; therefore thou liest.

First Clown. 'Tis a quick lie, sir ; 'twill away again, from me to you.

Hamlet. What man dost thou dig it for ?

First Clown. For no man, sir.

140 *Hamlet.* What woman, then ?

First Clown. For none, neither.

Hamlet. Who is to be buried in't ?

First Clown. One that was a woman, sir ; but, rest her soul, she's dead.

Hamlet. How absolute the knave is ! we must speak by the card, or equivocation will undo us. By the Lord, Horatio, these three years I have taken note of it ; the age is grown so picked that the toe of the peasant comes so near the heel of the courtier, he

150 galls his kibe. How long hast thou been a grave-maker ?

---

146. *By the card* (compass card), Exact to a point.
146. *Equivocation*, Ambiguity.   148. *Picked*, Fastidious.
150. *Kibe*, Chilblain.

First Clown. Of all the days i' the year, I came to't that day that our last king Hamlet overcame Fortinbras.

Hamlet. How long is that since ?

First Clown. Cannot you tell that ? every fool can tell that : it was the very day that young Hamlet was born ; he that is mad, and sent into England.

Hamlet. Ay, marry, why was he sent into England ?

160 *First Clown.* Why, because he was mad : he shall recover his wits there ; or, if he do not, it's no great matter there.

Hamlet. Why ?

First Clown. 'Twill not be seen in him there ; there the men are as mad as he.

Hamlet. How came he mad ?

First Clown. Very strangely, they say.

Hamlet. How strangely ?

First Clown. Faith, e'en with losing his wits.

170 *Hamlet.* Upon what ground ?

First Clown. Why, here in Denmark : I have been sexton here, man and boy, thirty years.

Hamlet. How long will a man lie i' the earth ere he rot ?

First Clown. I' faith, if he be not rotten before he die—as we have many corses now-a-days, that will scarce hold the laying in—he will last you some eight year or nine year : a tanner will last you nine year.

Hamlet. Why he more than another ?

180 *First Clown.* Why, sir, his hide is so tanned with his trade, that he will keep out water a great while ; and your water is a sore decayer of your dead body. Here's a skull now ; this skull has lain in the earth three and twenty years.

Hamlet. Whose was it ?

First Clown. A mad fellow's it was : whose do you think it was ?

Hamlet. Nay, I know not.

First Clown. A pestilence on him for a mad rogue !

190 a' poured a flagon of Rhenish on my head once.   This same skull, sir, was Yorick's skull, the king's jester.

    Hamlet. This ?

    First Clown. E'en that.

    Hamlet. Let me see. [*Takes the skull.*] Alas, poor Yorick ! I knew him, Horatio : a fellow of infinite jest, of most excellent fancy : he hath borne me on his back a thousand times ; and now, how abhorred in my imagination it is ! my gorge rises at it. Here hung those lips that I have kissed I know not how 200 oft. Where be your gibes now ? your gambols ? your songs ? your flashes of merriment, that were wont to set the table on a roar ? Not one now, to mock your own grinning ? quite chapfallen ? Now get you to my lady's chamber, and tell her, let her paint an inch thick, to this favour she must come ; make her laugh at that. Prithee, Horatio, tell me one thing.

    Horatio. What's that, my lord ?

    Hamlet. Dost thou think Alexander looked o' this fashion i' the earth ?

210   *Horatio.* E'en so ?

    Hamlet. And smelt so ? pah !

                             [*Puts down the skull.*]

    Horatio. E'en so, my lord.

    Hamlet. To what base uses we may return, Horatio ! Why may not imagination trace the noble dust of Alexander, till he find it stopping a bunghole ?

    Horatio. 'Twere to consider too curiously, to consider so.

    Hamlet. No, faith, not a jot ; but to follow him 220 thither with modesty enough, and likelihood to lead it : as thus : Alexander died, Alexander was buried, Alexander returneth into dust ; the dust is earth ; of earth we make loam ; and why of that loam, whereto he was converted, might they not stop a beer-barrel ?

---

190. *Rhenish*, Rhine wine.   205. *Favour*, Appearance.

Imperious Cæsar, dead and turn'd to clay,
Might stop a hole to keep the wind away :
O, that that earth, which kept the world in awe,
Should patch a wall to expel the winter's flaw !

But soft ! but soft ! aside : here comes the king,
[*Enter Priests, etc., in procession ; the corpse of
     Ophelia, Laertes and mourners following ; King,
     Queen, their trains, etc.*]
230 The queen, the courtiers : who is this they follow ?
And with such maimed rites ?   This doth betoken
The corse they follow did with desperate hand
Fordo it own life : 'twas of some estate.
Couch we awhile, and mark.
          [*They draw back so that they are not seen
               by the funeral party.*]

     Laertes. What ceremony else ?
     Hamlet.   That is Laertes,
A very noble youth : mark.
     Laertes. What ceremony else ?
     First Priest. Her obsequies have been as far en-
          larged
As we have warranty : her death was doubtful :
And, but that great command o'ersways the order,
240 She should in ground unsanctified have lodged
Till the last trumpet ; for charitable prayers,
Shards, flints, and pebbles should be thrown on her :
Yet here she is allow'd her virgin crants,
Her maiden strewments, and the bringing home
Of bell and burial.
     Laertes. Must there no more be done ?
     First Priest.   No more be done :
We should profane the service of the dead
To sing a requiem and such rest to her
As to peace-parted souls.

228. *Flaw,* Wind.   233. *Fordo,* Put an end to.
234. *Couch,* Lie in ambush.   242. *Shards,* Fragments of pottery.
243. *Crants,* Garland, wreath.
244. *Strewments,* Flowers strewn on a grave.

Laertes.   Lay her i' the earth :
250 And from her fair and unpolluted flesh
May violets spring ! [*The coffin is lowered into the
    grave.*] I tell thee, churlish priest,
A ministering angel shall my sister be,
When thou liest howling.
    Hamlet.   What, the fair Ophelia !
    Queen. Sweets to the sweet : farewell !
                    [*Scattering flowers in the grave.*]
I hoped thou shouldst have been my Hamlet's wife ;
I thought thy bride-bed to have deck'd, sweet maid,
And not have strew'd thy grave.
    Laertes.   O, treble woe
Fall ten times treble on that cursed head,
Whose wicked deed thy most ingenious sense
260 Deprived thee of !   Hold off the earth awhile,
Till I have caught her once more in mine arms :
                    [*Leaps into the grave.*]
Now pile your dust upon the quick and dead,
Till of this flat a mountain you have made,
To o'ertop old Pelion, or the skyish head
Of blue Olympus.
    Hamlet [advancing]. What is he whose grief
Bears such an emphasis ? whose phrase of sorrow
Conjures the wandering stars, and makes them stand
Like wonder-wounded hearers ?   This is I,
Hamlet the Dane.   [*Leaps into the grave.*]
    Laertes.   The devil take thy soul !
                    [*Grappling with him.*]
270 *Hamlet.* Thou pray'st not well.
I prithee, take thy fingers from my throat ;
For, though I am not splenitive and rash,
Yet have I something in me dangerous,
Which let thy wiseness fear : hold off thy hand.

253. *Liest howling,* In hell.
259. *Ingenious sense,* Delicately sensitive mind.
264. *Pelion,* A Greek mountain.   See page 157.
267. *Conjures,* Influences by magic.   *Wandering stars,* Planets.
272. *Splenitive,* Passionate.

King. Pluck them asunder.

Queen.　　　　　　　　　Hamlet, Hamlet !

All. Gentlemen,—

Horatio.　　　　　　　Good my lord, be quiet.

　　　　　[*The Attendants part them, and they come out*
　　　　　　of the grave.]

Hamlet. Why, I will fight with him upon this
　　theme

Until my eyelids will no longer wag.

Queen. O my son, what theme ?

280　*Hamlet.* I loved Ophelia : forty thousand brothers

Could not, with all their quantity of love,

Make up my sum.　What wilt thou do for her ?

King. O, he is mad, Laertes.

Queen. For love of God, forbear him.

Hamlet. 'Swounds, show me what thou'lt do :

Woo't weep ? woo't fight ? woo't fast ? woo't tear
　　thyself ?

Woo't drink up eisel ? eat a crocodile ?

I'll do't.　Dost thou come here to whine ?

To outface me with leaping in her grave ?

290 Be buried quick with her, and so will I :

And, if thou prate of mountains, let them throw

Millions of acres on us, till our ground,

Singeing his pate against the burning zone,

Make Ossa like a wart !　Nay, an thou'lt mouth,

I'll rant as well as thou.

Queen.　　　　　　　This is mere madness :

And thus awhile the fit will work on him ;

Anon, as patient as the female dove,

When that her golden couplets are disclosed,

His silence will sit drooping.

Hamlet.　　　　　　Hear you, sir ;

300 What is the reason that you use me thus ?

I loved you ever : but it is no matter :

287. *Eisel*, Vinegar (?).　See page 157.　　　290. *Quick*, Alive.
294. *Ossa*, A Greek mountain.　See page 157.
298. *Golden couplets are disclosed*, Two yellow chicks are hatched.

Let Hercules himself do what he may,
The cat will mew and dog will have his day.   [*Exit.*]
    King. I pray you, good Horatio, wait upon him.

                                    [*Exit Horatio.*]

[*To Laertes*] Strengthen your patience in our last
        night's speech ;
We'll put the matter to the present push.
Good Gertrude, set some watch over your son.
This grave shall have a living monument :
An hour of quiet shortly shall we see ;
310 Till then, in patience our proceeding be.   [*Exeunt.*]

SCENE II

A hall in the castle.

[*Enter Hamlet and Horatio.*]
    Hamlet. So much for this, sir : now shall you see
        the other ;
You do remember all the circumstance ?
    Horatio. Remember it, my lord !
    Hamlet. Sir, in my heart there was a kind of fight-
        ing,
That would not let me sleep ; methought I lay
Worse than the mutines in the bilboes.   Rashly,
And praised be rashness for it, let us know,
Our indiscretion sometimes serves us well,
When our deep plots do pall : and that should teach us
10 There's a divinity that shapes our ends,
Rough-hew them how we will,—
    Horatio.   That is most certain.
    Hamlet. Up from my cabin,
My sea-gown scarf'd about me, in the dark
Groped I to find out them ; had my desire,

306. *Present push,* Instant test.
6. *Mutines . . . bilboes,* Mutineers in fetters.   9. *Pall,* Fail.

Finger'd their packet, and in fine withdrew
To mine own room again ; making so bold,
My fears forgetting manners, to unseal
Their grand commission ; where I found, Horatio,—
O royal knavery !—an exact command,
20 Larded with many several sorts of reasons
Importing Denmark's health and England's too,
With, ho ! such bugs and goblins in my life,
That, on the supervise, no leisure bated,
No, not to stay the grinding of the axe,
My head should be struck off.

    Horatio.   Is't possible ?

    Hamlet. Here's the commission : read it at more
        leisure.
But wilt thou hear me how I did proceed ?

    Horatio. I beseech you.

    Hamlet. Being thus be-netted round with villanies,
30 Ere I could make a prologue to my brains,
They had begun the play—I sat me down,
Devised a new commission, wrote it fair :
I once did hold it, as our statists do,
A baseness to write fair, and labour'd much
How to forget that learning, but, sir, now
It did me yeoman's service : wilt thou know
The effect of what I wrote ?

    Horatio.   Ay, good my lord.

    Hamlet. An earnest conjuration from the king,
As England was his faithful tributary,
40 As love between them like the palm might flourish,
As peace should still her wheaten garland wear
And stand a comma 'tween their amities,
And many such-like "As"es of great charge,
That, on the view and knowing of these contents,
Without debatement further, more or less,
He should the bearers put to sudden death,
Not shriving-time allow'd.

23. *Supervise*, Reading.   *No leisure bated*, At once.
33. *Statists*, Politicians.   42. *Comma*, Connecting link (?).

Horatio.   How was this seal'd ?

Hamlet. Why, even in that was heaven ordinant.
I had my father's signet in my purse,
50 Which was the model of that Danish seal ;
Folded the writ up in form of the other,
Subscribed it, gave't the impression, placed it safely,
The changeling never known.   Now, the next day
Was our sea-fight ; and what to this was sequent
Thou know'st already.

Horatio. So Guildenstern and Rosencrantz go to't.

Hamlet. Why, man, they did make love to this
        employment ;
They are not near my conscience ; their defeat
Does by their own insinuation grow :
'Tis dangerous when the baser nature comes
60 Between the pass and fell incensed points
Of mighty opposites.

Horatio.   Why, what a king is this !

Hamlet. Does it not, think'st thee, stand me now
        upon—
He that hath kill'd my king, defiled my mother,
Popp'd in between the election and my hopes,
Thrown out his angle for my proper life,
And with such cozenage—is't not perfect conscience,
To quit him with this arm ? and is't not to be damn'd,
To let this canker of our nature come
In further evil ?

70   *Horatio.* It must shortly be known to him from
        England
What is the issue of the business there.

Hamlet. It will be short : the interim is mine ;
And a man's life's no more than to say " One."

---

50. *Model,* Copy.   57. *Defeat,* Ruin, destruction.
58. *Insinuation,* Artful intrusion.
60. *Pass,* Thrust.   *Points,* Sword-points.
62. *Stand me now upon,* Is it not incumbent on me ?
64. *Election,* Succession to the throne.
65. *Angle,* Fishing-hook.   *My proper,* My own.
66. *Cozenage,* Cheating.   68. *Canker,* " Plague-spot " (the King).

But I am very sorry, good Horatio,
That to Laertes I forgot myself ;
For, by the image of my cause, I see
The portraiture of his : I'll court his favours :
But, sure, the bravery of his grief did put me
Into a towering passion.

    Horatio.   Peace ! who comes here ?

    [*Enter Osric. On seeing Hamlet he stops short,
        takes off his hat and bows repeatedly, with
        exaggerated politeness.*]

80   *Osric.* Your lordship is right welcome back to
Denmark.

    Hamlet. I humbly thank you, sir. [*Aside to Hor-
atio.*] Dost know this water-fly ?

    Horatio. No, my good lord.

    Hamlet. Thy state is the more gracious ; for 'tis a
vice to know him. He hath much land, and fertile :
let a beast be lord of beasts, and his crib shall stand
at the king's mess : 'tis a chough ; but, as I say,
spacious in the possession of dirt.

90   *Osric* [*approaching*]. Sweet lord, if your lordship
were at leisure, I should impart a thing to you from
his majesty.

    Hamlet. I will receive it, sir, with all diligence of
spirit. Put your bonnet to his right use ; 'tis for the
head.

    Osric. I thank your lordship, it is very hot.

    Hamlet. No, believe me, 'tis very cold ; the wind is
northerly.

    Osric. It is indifferent cold, my lord, indeed.

100   *Hamlet.* But yet methinks it is very sultry and hot
for my complexion.

    Osric. Exceedingly, my lord ; it is very sultry,—as
'twere,—I cannot tell how. But, my lord, his majesty bade me signify to you that he has laid a great
wager on your head : sir, this is the matter,—

78. *Bravery*, Ostentatious display.
88. *Chough*, Jackdaw (most probably).

Hamlet. I beseech you, remember—
          [*Hamlet moves him to put on his hat.*]
Osric. Nay, good my lord ; for mine ease, in good faith. Sir, here is newly come to court Laertes ; believe me, an absolute gentleman, full of most excel-
110 lent differences, of very soft society and great show-ing : indeed, to speak feelingly of him, he is the card or calendar of gentry, for you shall find in him the continent of what part a gentleman would see.

Hamlet [*mimicking Osric's affected speech*]. Sir, his definement suffers no perdition in you ; though, I know, to divide him inventorially would dizzy the arithmetic of memory, and yet but yaw neither, in respect of his quick sail. But, in the verity of extol-ment, I take him to be a soul of great article ; and his
120 infusion of such dearth and rareness, as, to make true diction of him, his semblable is his mirror ; and who else would trace him, his umbrage, nothing more.

Osric. Your lordship speaks most infallibly of him.
Hamlet. The concernancy, sir ? why do we wrap the gentleman in our more rawer breath ?

Osric [*beaten at his own game and becoming be-wildered*]. Sir ?

Horatio. Is't not possible to understand in another tongue ? You will do't, sir, really.

Hamlet. What imports the nomination of this
130 gentleman ?

Osric. Of Laertes ?

Horatio. His purse is empty already ; all's golden words are spent.

Hamlet. Of him, sir.

Osric. I know you are not ignorant—

111. *Card, calendar*, Guide, directory.
113. *Continent*, Sum, summary.   115. *Perdition*, Loss.
117. *Yaw* (used of a ship), Move unsteadily, diverge from the course.
119. *Article*, Importance, scope.
120. *Infusion*, The qualities infused in him. *Dearth*, Dearness.
121. *His semblable*, etc. See page 158.
124. *Concernancy*, How does this concern us ?

Hamlet. I would you did, sir ; yet, in faith, if you did, it would not much approve me. Well, sir ?

Osric. You are not ignorant of what excellence Laertes is—

140 *Hamlet.* I dare not confess that, lest I should compare with him in excellence ; but, to know a man well, were to know himself.

Osric. I mean, sir, for his weapon ; but in the imputation laid on him by them, in his meed he's unfellowed.

Hamlet. What's his weapon ?

Osric. Rapier and dagger.

Hamlet. That's two of his weapons : but, well.

Osric. The king, sir, hath wagered with him six 150 Barbary horses : against the which he has imponed, as I take it, six French rapiers and poniards, with their assigns, as girdle, hangers, and so : three of the carriages, in faith, are very dear to fancy, very responsive to the hilts, most delicate carriages, and of very liberal conceit.

Hamlet. What call you the carriages ?

Horatio. I knew you must be edified by the margent ere you had done.

Osric. The carriages, sir, are the hangers.

160 *Hamlet.* The phrase would be more german to the matter, if we could carry cannon by our sides : I would it might be hangers till then. But, on : six Barbary horses against six French swords, their assigns, and three liberal-conceited carriages ; that's the French bet against the Danish. Why is this " imponed," as you call it ?

Osric. The king, sir, hath laid, that in a dozen passes between yourself and him, he shall not exceed you

---

144. *Meed*, Merit.   150. *Imponed*, Impawned, wagered (?).
153. *Very responsive*, Closely corresponding.
155. *Liberal conceit*, Tasteful design.
157. *Edified by the margent*, Instructed by the explanatory notes in the margin (frequent in old books).
160. *German*, Appropriate.

three hits : he hath laid on twelve for nine ; and it
170 would come to immediate trial, if your lordship would
vouchsafe the answer.

Hamlet. How if I answer " No " ?

Osric. I mean, my lord, the opposition of your
person in trial.

Hamlet. Sir, I will walk here in the hall : if it
please his majesty, 'tis the breathing time of day with
me ; let the foils be brought, the gentleman willing,
and the king hold his purpose, I will win for him an I
can ; if not, I will gain nothing but my shame and the
180 odd hits.

Osric. Shall I re-deliver you e'en so ?

Hamlet. To this effect, sir ; after what flourish
your nature will.

Osric. I commend my duty to your lordship.

Hamlet. Yours, yours. [*Exit Osric.*] He does well to
commend it himself ; there are no tongues else for's
turn.

Horatio. This lapwing runs away with the shell on
his head.

190   *Hamlet.* Thus has he—and many more of the same
breed that I know the drossy age dotes on—only got
the tune of the time and outward habit of encounter ;
a kind of yesty collection, which carries them through
and through the most fond and winnowed opinions ;
and do but blow them to their trial, the bubbles
are out.

[*Enter a Lord.*]

Lord. My lord, his majesty commended him to you
by young Osric, who brings back to him, that you
attend him in the hall : he sends to know if your
200 pleasure hold to play with Laertes, or that you will
take longer time.

Hamlet. I am constant to my purposes ; they
follow the king's pleasure : if his fitness speaks, mine

176. *Breathing time,* Time for exercise.   191. *Drossy,* Frivolous.
193. *Yesty,* Frothy.   See page 159.

is ready ; now or whensoever, provided I be so able
as now.

Lord. The king and queen and all are coming down.

Hamlet. In happy time.

Lord. The queen desires you to use some gentle
entertainment to Laertes before you fall to play.

210   *Hamlet.* She well instructs me.   [*Exit Lord.*]

Horatio. You will lose this wager, my lord.

Hamlet. I do not think so : since he went into
France, I have been in continual practice ; I shall win
at the odds.   But thou wouldst not think how ill all's
here about my heart : but it is no matter.

Horatio. Nay, good my lord,—

Hamlet. It is but foolery ; but it is such a kind of
gain-giving, as would perhaps trouble a woman.

Horatio. If your mind dislike anything, obey it : I
220 will forestall their repair hither, and say you are
not fit.

Hamlet. Not a whit, we defy augury : there's a
special providence in the fall of a sparrow.   If it be
now, 'tis not to come ; if it be not to come, it will be
now ; if it be not now, yet it will come : the readiness
is all : since no man has aught of what he leaves, what
is't to leave betimes ?

[*Enter King, Queen, Laertes, Lords, Osric, and
Attendants with foils, etc.*]

King. Come, Hamlet, come, and take this hand
          from me.

          [*The King puts Laertes' hand into Hamlet's.*]

Hamlet. Give me your pardon, sir : I've done you
          wrong ;

230 But pardon't, as you are a gentleman.

This presence knows,

And you must needs have heard, how I am
          punish'd

With sore distraction.   What I have done,

218. *Gain-giving*, Misgiving, presentiment.
227. *Betimes*, Early.   See page 159.

That might your nature, honour and exception
Roughly awake, I here proclaim was madness.
Was't Hamlet wrong'd Laertes ? Never Hamlet :
If Hamlet from himself be ta'en away,
And when he's not himself does wrong Laertes,
Then Hamlet does it not, Hamlet denies it.
240 Who does it, then ? His madness : if't be so,
Hamlet is of the faction that is wrong'd ;
His madness is poor Hamlet's enemy.
Sir, in this audience,
Let my disclaiming from a purposed evil
Free me so far in your most generous thoughts,
That I have shot mine arrow o'er the house,
And hurt my brother.
    Laertes.   I am satisfied in nature,
Whose motive, in this case, should stir me most
To my revenge : but in my terms of honour
250 I stand aloof ; and will no reconcilement,
Till by some elder masters, of known honour,
I have a voice and precedent of peace,
To keep my name ungored. But till that time,
I do receive your offer'd love like love,
And will not wrong it.
    Hamlet.   I embrace it freely ;
And will this brother's wager frankly play.
Give us the foils. Come on.
    Laertes.   Come, one for me.
    Hamlet. I'll be your foil, Laertes : in mine igno-
        rance
Your skill shall, like a star i' the darkest night,
260 Stick fiery off indeed.
    Laertes.   You mock me, sir.
    Hamlet. No, by this hand.
    King. Give them the foils, young Osric. Cousin
        Hamlet,
You know the wager ?

---

234. *Exception*, Disapproval.
260. *Stick fiery off*, Stand out brilliantly.

Hamlet.   Very well, my lord ;
Your grace hath laid the odds o' the weaker side.
King. I do not fear it ; I have seen you both :
But since he is better'd, we have therefore odds.
Laertes. This is too heavy, let me see another.
Hamlet. This likes me well.   These foils have all a
          length ?   [*They prepare to play.*]
Osric. Ay, my good lord.
270 *King.* Set me the stoups of wine upon that table.
If Hamlet give the first or second hit,
Or quit in answer of the third exchange,
Let all the battlements their ordnance fire ;
The king shall drink to Hamlet's better breath ;
And in the cup an union shall he throw,
Richer than that which four successive kings
In Denmark's crown have worn.   Give me the cups ;
And let the kettle to the trumpet speak,
The trumpet to the cannoneer without,
280 The cannons to the heavens, the heavens to earth,
" Now the king drinks to Hamlet."   Come, begin :
And you, the judges, bear a wary eye.
Hamlet. Come on, sir.
Laertes.   Come, my lord. [*They play.*]
Hamlet.   One.
Laertes.   No.
Hamlet.   Judgment.
Osric. A hit, a very palpable hit.
Laertes.   Well ; again.
King. Stay ; give me drink.   Hamlet, this pearl is
          thine ;
Here's to thy health.
          [*Trumpets sound, and cannon shot off within.*]
                    Give him the cup.
Hamlet. I'll play this bout first ; set it by awhile.

---

266. *Better'd*, Improved (?) ; trained by better masters (?).
275. *Union*, A fine pearl which would dissolve : an old custom.   In
     'this case the " pearl " is really the poison.
278. *Kettle*, Kettledrum.

Come.   [*They play.*]

Hamlet. Another hit ; what say you ?

Laertes. A touch, a touch, I do confess.

290   *King.* Our son shall win.

Queen.   He's fat, and scant of breath.

Here, Hamlet, take my napkin, rub thy brows :

[*She gives Hamlet her handkerchief, and then takes up
the poisoned cup.*]

The queen carouses to thy fortune, Hamlet.

Hamlet [*acknowledging her courtesy*]. Good madam !

King.   Gertrude, do not drink.

Queen. I will, my lord ; I pray you, pardon me.

King [*aside*]. It is the poison'd cup : it is too late.

Hamlet. I dare not drink yet, madam ; by and by.

Queen. Come, let me wipe thy face.

Laertes. My lord, I'll hit him now.

King.   I do not think't.

Laertes [*aside*]. And yet 'tis almost 'gainst my
conscience.

300   *Hamlet.* Come, for the third, Laertes : you but
dally ;

I pray you, pass with your best violence ;

I am afeard you make a wanton of me.

Laertes [*incensed*]. Say you so ? come on.

[*They play.*]

Osric. Nothing, neither way.

Laertes. Have at you now !

[*Laertes wounds Hamlet, who gives ground for a
moment, then attacks fiercely and disarms his
opponent. Snatching up Laertes' rapier he
throws down his own, which Laertes takes up.*]

King [*in alarm*]. Part them ; they are incensed.

Hamlet. Nay, come, again.

[*He attacks Laertes and wounds him with the poisoned
rapier. The Queen falls.*]

Osric.   Look to the queen there, ho !

290. *Fat*, (?) Out of condition. See page 159.
302. *Wanton*, Plaything. (You are not doing your best.)

Horatio. They bleed on both sides. [*Anxiously going
    to Hamlet's support.*] How is it, my lord ?
Osric. How is't, Laertes ?
Laertes. Why, as a woodcock to mine own springe,
    Osric ;
310 I am justly kill'd with mine own treachery.
Hamlet. How does the queen ?
King.   She swounds to see them bleed.
Queen [*half raising herself*]. No, no, the drink, the
    drink,—O my dear Hamlet,—
The drink, the drink ! I am poison'd.   [*She dies.*]
Hamlet. O villany ! Ho ! let the door be lock'd :
Treachery !   Seek it out.
Laertes [*reeling against the table*]. It is here, Hamlet :
    Hamlet, thou art slain ;
No medicine in the world can do thee good ;
In thee there is not half an hour of life ;
The treacherous instrument is in thy hand,
320 Unbated and envenom'd : the foul practice
Hath turn'd itself on me ; lo, here I lie,
Never to rise again : thy mother's poison'd :
I can no more : the king, the king's to blame.
Hamlet. The point envenom'd too !
Then, venom, to thy work.   [*He stabs the King.*]
All. Treason ! treason !
King. O, yet defend me, friends ; I am but hurt.
Hamlet [*forcing the King to drink some of the
    poisoned wine*]. Here, thou incestuous, mur-
    derous, damned Dane,
Drink off this potion.   Is thy union here ?
330 Follow my mother.
                [*The King falls beside the throne and dies.*]
Laertes.   He is justly served ;
It is a poison temper'd by himself.
Exchange forgiveness with me, noble Hamlet :

309. *Springe,* Snare.
320. *Unbated,* Not blunted (with the usual button). *Practice,*
    Stratagem.

Mine and my father's death come not upon thee,
Nor thine on me !   [*Dies.*]
    Hamlet. Heaven make thee free of it ! I follow
        thee.
I am dead, Horatio.   Wretched queen, adieu !
You that look pale and tremble at this chance,
That are but mutes or audience to this act,
Had I but time—as this fell sergeant, death,
340 Is strict in his arrest—O, I could tell you—
But let it be.   Horatio, I am dead ;
Thou livest ; report me and my cause aright
To the unsatisfied.
    Horatio [*supporting Hamlet in his arms*]. Never
        believe it :
I am more an antique Roman than a Dane
Here's yet some liquor left.
                        [*He seizes the poisoned cup.*]
    Hamlet.   As thou'rt a man,
Give me the cup : let go ; by heaven, I'll have't.
        [*Wresting it from Horatio, he throws it down.*]
O good Horatio, what a wounded name,
Things standing thus unknown, shall live behind
        me !
If thou didst ever hold me in thy heart,
350 Absent thee from felicity awhile,
And in this harsh world draw thy breath in pain,
To tell my story.   [*March afar off, and shot within.*]
What warlike noise is this ?
    Osric. Young Fortinbras, with conquest come from
        Poland,
To the ambassadors of England gives
This warlike volley.
    Hamlet.   O, I die, Horatio ;
The potent poison quite o'er-crows my spirit :
I cannot live to hear the news from England ;

---

339. *Fell*, Fierce, cruel. *Sergeant*, Sheriff's officer, who arrested
        debtors and other offenders.
357. *O'ercrows*, Overpowers, triumphs over.

But I do prophesy the election lights
360 On Fortinbras : he has my dying voice ;
So tell him, with the occurrents, more and less,
Which have solicited.   The rest is silence.   [*He dies.*]
    Horatio. Now cracks a noble heart.   Good night,
        sweet prince ;
And flights of angels sing thee to thy rest !
Why does the drum come hither ?
    [*Horatio lays Hamlet's body at the foot of the throne.*
       There is the sound of a march.   Enter Fortin-
       bras, the English Ambassadors, and others.]
    Fortinbras. Where is this sight ?
    Horatio.   What is it ye would see ?
If aught of woe or wonder, cease your search.
    Fortinbras. This quarry cries on havoc.   O proud
        death,
What feast is toward in thine eternal cell,
370 That thou so many princes at a shot
So bloodily hast struck ?
    First Ambassador.   The sight is dismal ;
And our affairs from England come too late :
The ears are senseless that should give us hearing,
To tell him his commandment is fulfill'd,
That Rosencrantz and Guildenstern are dead :
Where should we have our thanks ?
                      [*He looks at the dead King.*]
    Horatio.   Not from his mouth,
Had it the ability of life to thank you :
He never gave commandment for their death.
But since, so jump upon this bloody question,
380 You from the Polack wars, and you from England,
Are here arrived, give order that these bodies
High on a stage be placed to the view ;
And let me speak to the yet unknowing world
How these things came about : so shall you hear
Of carnal, bloody, and unnatural acts,

      362. *Solicited,* Prompted (my actions).
      368. *Quarry,* Heap of slain.   See page 160.

Of accidental judgments, casual slaughters,
Of depths put on by cunning and forced cause,
And, in this upshot, purposes mistook
Fall'n on the inventors' heads : all this can I
390 Truly deliver.
     Fortinbras.   Let us haste to hear it,
And call the noblest to the audience.
For me, with sorrow I embrace my fortune :
I have some rights of memory in this kingdom,
Which now to claim my vantage doth invite me.
     Horatio. Of that I shall have also cause to speak,
And from his mouth whose voice will draw on more :
But let this same be presently perform'd,
Even while men's minds are wild ; lest more mis-
        chance,
On plots and errors, happen.
     Fortinbras.   Let four captains
400 Bear Hamlet, like a soldier, to the stage ;
For he was likely, had he been put on,
To have proved most royally : and, for his passage,
The soldiers' music and the rites of war
Speak loudly for him.
Take up the bodies : such a sight as this
Becomes the field, but here shows much amiss.
Go, bid the soldiers shoot.
    [*A dead march.* *Exeunt, bearing off the dead bodies ;*
      after which a peal of ordnance is shot off.]

                387. *Put on,* Instigated.
                393. *Of memory,* Remembered.

Notes are often necessary, but they are necessary evils. Let him that is yet unacquainted with the powers of SHAKESPEARE, *and who desires to feel the highest pleasure that the drama can give, read every play from the first scene to the last, with utter negligence of all his commentators. When his fancy is once on the wing, let it not stoop at correction or explanation. . . . Let him read on through brightness and obscurity, through integrity and corruption ; let him preserve his comprehension of the dialogue and his interest in the fable. And when the pleasures of novelty have ceased, let him attempt exactness, and read the commentators.*

SAMUEL JOHNSON.

" Preface to Shakespeare," 1765.

*I dreamt last night that Shakespeare's ghost
Sat for a Civil Service post.
The English papers of the year
Contained a question on* KING LEAR,
*Which Shakespeare answered very badly
Because he hadn't studied* BRADLEY.

GUY BOAS.

" Lays of Learning," 1926.

ADDITIONAL NOTES

Act I. Scene I.

Line 42. *Thou art a scholar ; speak to it, Horatio.*
A scholar could speak to the Ghost in Latin, the
language used in exorcising spirits.

63. *Sledded Polacks.* It has been suggested that
the correct reading is *pole-axe* (as in the Fourth
Folio Shakespeare of 1685), and that *sledded* means
weighted. (*Cf.* " sledge-hammer.") Which reading
is better poetry ? Which is better sense ? Remember
that " parle " means " parley," and that the King
apparently had his visor up. The Second Quarto has
sleaded pollax, and the First Folio *sledded Pollax*.

114. *Ere the mightiest Julius fell.* See Shakespeare's
Julius Cæsar, Act II, Scene ii. Comets and other
unusual phenomena were long held to be warnings of
disasters to come.

The grammatical difficulty of this passage is
obvious. A line or more may have been lost.

Act I. Scene II.

Line 65. *A little more than kin and less than kind.*
More than kin because twice related, as uncle and
as stepfather ; less than kind (natural) because this
relationship is unnatural. A pun, because " kind "
was pronounced " kinn'd " in Shakespeare's time.
Punning was then regarded as very witty ; the
satirical and epigrammatic force of his first speech

is apparently meant to introduce Hamlet as a man of high intellect. In his next speech " sun " may be a pun on " son."

113. *School in Wittenberg*. The German university which Martin Luther had made famous. It was founded in 1502, long after Hamlet's time, but Shakespeare and his contemporaries never troubled about such petty anachronisms as this.

216. *It head*. The modern form "its," which did not appear in any play of Shakespeare's published during his lifetime, came gradually into use during the seventeenth century. Elizabethan writers generally used " his." See Henry Bradley : *The Making of English*, pages 56–57.

ACT I. SCENE IV.

Line 16. *More honour'd in the breach* . . . This line has become proverbial, and is nearly always given a wrong meaning. In what way ?

36. *The dram of eale Doth all the noble substance of a doubt To his own scandal*. This very difficult passage is probably corrupt, and over a hundred emendations have been suggested ! See the *Variorum Shakespeare* and *Cambridge Shakespeare*.

" Of a dout " is most suspect. Perhaps it should read " often dout " (= put out, extinguish), which would give the meaning, " The drop of evil doth all the noble substance often extinguish, and bring it to its own evil condition." Other emendations include " oft abate," " out o' doubt."

Professor Dowden suggests that " doth . . . Scandal " should be taken as the verb, and the passage read, " Out of a mere doubt or suspicion the dram of evil degrades in reputation all the noble substance to its own substance."

Another possibility is that the sentence is not

corrupt at all, but only incomplete, Hamlet being interrupted by Horatio's exclamation.

Lines 17–38 do not appear in the First Folio or First Quarto (see pages 167–171). Would the scene gain or lose dramatically by their omission?

ACT I. SCENE v.

Line 80. *O horrible* . . . This line is given to Hamlet by several editors, and by Garrick, Sir Henry Irving, and other actors, although there is no authority in the early editions. Do you think it is better spoken by Hamlet?

ACT II. SCENE I.

Line 63. *God be wi' you.* The First Folio has " God buy you,"—probably the Elizabethan pronunciation. The phrase is in process of transition to our modern form, " Good-bye."

113–114. *Which, being kept close, might move More grief to hide than hate to utter love.* Probably, " concealing this love-secret of Hamlet's might cause more grief than revealing it would cause hatred (in Hamlet?)." The obscurity is perhaps due to the effort to make a rhyming couplet for the end of the scene.

ACT II. SCENE II.

Line 109 *ff.* Hamlet's letter. " *Beautified* " Polonius may regard as " vile " because of its ambiguity. The verse and the letter are in the courtly style of Shakespeare's time, and there is no reason to doubt their sincerity.

182. *Being a god kissing carrion.* " If a dead dog is corrupted by the sun [the ' god '], how much more

your daughter by me."—Hamlet's ironical justifica-
tion of Polonius' attempt to separate him from
Ophelia. But the Second Quarto and Folios have
" good kissing," which would probably mean " good
for kissing (by the sun)." Either reading may be
correct. The emendation, a famous one, was made
by Warburton.

263. *Then are our beggars' bodies, and our monarchs
and outstretched heroes the beggars' shadows*. " If
ambition is but a shadow, something beyond ambition
must be the substance from which it is thrown. If
ambition, represented by a king, is a shadow, the
antitype of ambition, represented by a beggar, must
be the opposite of the shadow, that is, the substance "
(Bucknill). But Hamlet is playing with words, for his
own amusement or the mystification of Rosencrantz
and Guildenstern ; there may be no exact meaning.

328. *Humorous man*. Like many other passages in
Shakespeare, this refers to the old medical theory that
the composition of the human body included four
" humours " or fluids—blood, phlegm, choler (or
yellow bile), and melancholy (or black bile). Predominance of one of these caused the temperament
(= mixture) to be sanguine, phlegmatic, choleric, or
melancholy ; excessive predominance caused illness.
Hence " humour " sometimes meant a particular
characteristic. Shakespeare's friend, Ben Jonson,
wrote " comedies of humours," in which the characters are little more than personifications of such
traits as greed, boasting, jealousy, etc.

338–369. *I think their inhibition*, etc. This conversation has little meaning or value to the modern
audience, especially as much of it is in contemporary
slang—the slang satirized later in Act V., Scene ii.
(pages 135–136).

It refers to the rivalry between the professional
companies of adult actors, who played in the public
theatres, *common stages*, outside the City, and the

schoolboy companies, the *children* of St. Paul's, the Chapel Royal, etc., who acted in the so-called " private " theatres. The latter were for a time so much *the fashion* that the adult players found their audiences depleted, and were compelled to *travel*. This is probably the *inhibition* mentioned, but they may have been under a legal prohibition also. The rivalry was intense when this passage was written, about 1600–1601. Shakespeare, who was a good business man, was on both sides. He was a shareholder in the Globe, one of the chief public theatres, and a member of the Lord Chamberlain's men who acted there ; he also had shares in the most important " private " theatre, the Blackfriars. Ben Jonson played a leading part in this " war of the theatres."

There are many such topical allusions in plays of the time.

There is a contemporary comment on the success of the " children " in *Jack Drum's Entertainment,* 1601 :

> " I saw the children of Powles last night ;
> And troth they pleased me pretty, pretty well,
> The apes, in time, will do it handsomely. . . .
> I like the audience that frequenteth there
> With much applause : a man shall not be choak'd
> With the stench of garlick, nor be pasted
> To the balmy jacket of a beer-brewer. . . .
> 'Tis a good gentle audience. . . ."

406. *Scene individable*, etc. Much has been written, to little purpose, about the "Three Unities," especially by the so-called " classical " critics of France and England in the sixteenth, seventeenth, and eighteenth centuries. From a misunderstanding of a passage in Aristotle's *Poetics*, and deductions from Greek dramatic practice, it was sometimes maintained that a playwright *must* observe these unities : Unity of Time, limiting the action of a play to twenty-four hours, or less ; Unity of Place, limiting

the scene to one spot, or at least to a small area ; Unity of Action, limiting the plot to one story, with no sub-plot. Observation of these "laws" often strengthens a play, but they are not essential.

"Scene individable" observes the unities. "Poem unlimited" breaks them. These players are equally good in either.

454. *Æneas' tale to Dido.* The "speech" is based on a passage in Virgil's *Æneid*, Book II., in which Æneas tells Dido, Queen of Carthage, the story of the sack of Troy by the Greeks. *Priam* was the aged King of Troy ; *Hecuba* his wife, mother of Hector ; *Pyrrhus*, son of Achilles. The armour of *Mars*, the god of war, was forged by the *Cyclops*, the giant assistants of Vulcan, god of fire.

The whole speech is written in the melodramatic style which was popular when Shakespeare first began to write. Some critics think it is meant as a burlesque of the style.

530. *The abstract and brief chronicles of the time.* "In the Elizabethan age the drama, often dealing with and satirizing contemporary life, had an influence similar to that of the newspaper and the novel on the life of the present day."

ACT III. SCENE I.

Line 56. *To be, or not to be.* To what does this refer ?

59. *Take arms against a sea of troubles.* A mixed metaphor, or a corrupt line, or a reference to the old story that Celtic warriors used to show their courage by armed combats with the waves.

68–69. *There's the respect . . . long life.* There's the consideration that makes the miserable bear life so long.

79–80. *From whose bourn No traveller returns.*

" Then how about the Ghost ? " asked Theobald. What is the answer ?

130–131. *Where's your father ?—At home, my lord.* Is it possible that Ophelia thinks she is telling the truth ?

147–148. *Nickname . . . your ignorance,* call things by immodest names, and then profess childish ignorance of what you have said.

150. *All but one shall live.* Is this consciously aimed at the eavesdropping King ?

Act III. Scene ii.

Line 99. *You played once i' the university.* University plays, in Latin and English, were an important part of Tudor drama. A Latin play on Cæsar's death was acted at Oxford in 1582. *Hamlet* was acted at both Oxford and Cambridge. What other references to Julius Cæsar are there in *Hamlet* ?

104. *Capitol.* This mistake appears also in Shakespeare's *Julius Cæsar.* The murder took place in Pompey's Theatre.

128. *The hobby-horse is forgot.* The hobby-horse appeared in May games and morris-dances—" a figure of a horse made of light material and fastened round the waist of a performer," who thus represented both horse and rider. This reference may be a hit at the Puritans, who were trying to abolish these dances, and to close all the theatres.

128–129. *The Dumb Show.* See page 188. *Phœbus' cart,* the sun-god's chariot. *Neptune's salt wash,* the sea. *Tellus' orbed ground,* the earth. *Hymen,* Greek and Roman god of marriage.

230. *Gonzago.* There is a possible historical foundation for the story of the play ; in 1538 the Duke of Urbano, in Italy, was murdered by a Luigi Gonzaga, who dropped poison into his ear. If the exact story

is extant it has never been found. "Duke" may be an oversight. The First Quarto has "Duke" and "Duchess" throughout, and "Albertus" for "Gonzago."

Note how the rhymed verse distinguishes the "play within the play."

236. *Chorus*, acting as interpreter. *Cf.* the choruses in *Henry V*.

260. *Why, let the stricken deer* . . . The verse is probably quoted from a ballad.

Act III. Scene iv.

Lines 56–58. *Hyperion*, the sun-god (Greek). *Jove*, chief of the gods. *Mars*, war-god. *Mercury*, messenger of the gods, who had winged heels.

This passage is ludicrously misquoted by Mrs. Malaprop in Sheridan's *The Rivals*, Act IV., Scene ii.

168. *And either the devil*, is the reading of the Second Quarto. To complete the sense, "master" has been added by some editors, because the Fourth Quarto has, "And Maister the devill." In the *Globe* text a blank is left.

Lines 160–164a, 166b–169a, 179a appear in the Second Quarto, but not the First Folio.

Act IV. Scene i.

Line 40. *So, haply, slander*. Many editors insert this. It is not in the *Globe* text. Lines 41–44a, *whose whisper . . . woundless air*, are not in the First Folio ; they are taken from the Second Quarto.

Act IV. Scene iv.

Line 27. *This is the imposthume of much wealth and peace*. "Such a senseless war is a disease caused by too much wealth and pride."

ADDITIONAL NOTES

32. *How all occasions*, etc. Is there anything in this soliloquy which reminds you of a passage in Tennyson's *Morte D'Arthur*?

ACT IV. SCENE V.

Ophelia's songs are snatches of old ballads. Music for them is given in the Variorum Shakespeare edition of *Hamlet* (Lippincott).

Line 41. *The owl was a baker's daughter.* An allusion to an old Gloucestershire legend about a selfish girl who begrudged giving bread to Christ, and was changed into an owl.

48. *St. Valentine's Day* (Feb. 14) used to be widely observed in England. See Sam Weller's Valentine in *Pickwick Papers*.

Ophelia's song alludes to the old custom of the first girl seen by a man on this day being considered his Valentine, or true-love.

86. *Switzers,* Swiss mercenary troops. "Law, logicke, and the Switzers may be hired to fight for anybody."—Thomas Nashe, 1594.

145–147. *Nature is fine . . . it loves.* "Nature is delicate (or accomplished) in love, and sends Ophelia's sanity after Polonius as a precious token (or sample) of itself."—Dowden.

164–169. *Fennel* (supposed to clear the sight), for flattery. *Columbine*, ingratitude (?). *Rue*, for sorrow and repentance. (Perhaps the *difference* is that Ophelia is to wear hers for sorrow, the Queen for repentance.) *Daisy*, for dissembling, treachery. *Violets*, for faithfulness.

Do you agree that Ophelia gives the flowers to the persons named in the stage directions, or would you suggest a different distribution?

Act IV. Scene VII.

Line 126. *Sanctuarize*. Some shrines, etc., were sanctuaries which protected from the law or from private revenge any criminal who took refuge in them.

168. *Crow-flowers*, buttercups. *Long purples*, purple orchis. Did the Queen stand by and watch Ophelia drown?

182. *Too much of water*, etc. The Elizabethans admired such quibbles, and Shakespeare could never resist them. Why does this one seem to us to strike such a false note?

185. *When these . . . will be out*. When these tears are shed, the weakness in me will all be gone.

Act V. Scene I.

Line 66. *In youth*, etc. The gravedigger's songs are his blundering versions of parts of a song by Lord Vaux, in *Tottel's Miscellany*, 1557.

Collections of songs were very popular in Shakespeare's time; this was the great age of English music.

The " O's " and " A's " may represent the clown's grunts as he digs!

104–115. *Quiddities*, subtleties. *Quillets*, verbal niceties. *Statutes*, *recognizances*, bonds. *Fines*, *double vouchers*, *recoveries*, terms connected with the purchase of land. *Indentures*, agreements. Shakespeare himself was buying land and houses about this time: one can imagine him stringing together all these terms with sarcastic satisfaction.

113–115. *Fine*, used punningly in four different senses: 1. end; 2. legal process; 3. elegant; 4. small.

123. *Assurance*, another pun: 1. certainty; 2. conveyance by deeds.

ADDITIONAL NOTES

147. *These three years.* No convincing explanation of this reference appears to have been offered.

172. *Thirty years.* Compare line 157. Does it surprise you to find that Hamlet is thirty years old? If so, why? See the note on "fat," page 159, below.

In the First Quarto Yorick has been dead "this dozen yeare," instead of twenty-three (line 184), and the other time-references do not appear.

208. *Alexander* the Great. "Perhaps Shakespeare thought of Alexander's beauty and sweet smell as well as of his conquests" (Dowden). These personal characteristics are emphasized in Plutarch's *Lives*, which Shakespeare knew in North's translation.

This famous Macedonian conqueror extended his empire as far as India, in the fourth century A.D.

243. *Crants.* "The crants were garlands which it was usual to make of white paper, and to hang up in the church on the occasion of a young girl's funeral. Some of these were hanging up in Flamborough Church, Yorkshire, as late as 1850" (Hardiman). "Crants" may be singular.

264. *Pelion, Olympus,* mountains in Greece. Olympus was the home of the gods. When the Titans made war upon the gods they piled Pelion on the top of Ossa (another mountain near by), and both on the lower slopes of Olympus, in order to scale the abode of the gods.

287. *Eisel.* Another famous textual crux. The Second Quarto has *esill*, the First Folio *esile*. Theobald, an eighteenth-century editor who had a genius for emendation, suggested that the word should be eisel (= vinegar), or that it was the name of a river, possibly "*Yssel*, in the German Flanders." There has been much discussion of this: the Variorum edition has four pages of notes in small type on the word. *Eisel*, vinegar, is now generally accepted. Eisel was "associated with gall as the bitter drink

offered to Christ " ; it was thought that it " hurteth them that be sorrowful." *Drink up* may mean no more than " drink."

308. *Living monument.* " Living " means " enduring," and the Queen would understand it so. " Laertes would be cognizant of the deeper meaning, by which the life of Hamlet is menaced."

ACT V. SCENE II.

Line 22. *With, ho ! such bugs and goblins in my life.* " With the suggestion of such terrors and perils if I am allowed to live " (C. H. Herford). Other explanations have been offered. *Bugs* = bugbears.

36. *Yeoman's service,* now proverbial for good and faithful service. The yeomen, small freeholders, were a large part of the infantry of English armies, " the good archers in times past, and the stable troop of footmen that affraide all France."

43. *" As "es,* quibbles on " asses." " As " was pronounced " ass " in Warwickshire, Shakespeare's native county.

53. *Changeling,* generally used for a child left by fairies in exchange for one stolen.

Osric is a caricature of the type of Elizabethan courtier who adopted a highly artificial and affected mode of speech. (Lyly's euphuism was one such mode.) With characteristic eagerness and quickness Hamlet mimics this style, and soon bewilders Osric's limited intelligence. *Concernancy, imponed,* and other words in this dialogue, do not occur elsewhere in Shakespeare. *Imponed* probably represents Osric's pronunciation of " impawned."

In lines 127–128 Horatio is probably suggesting that Osric should speak plain English.

See page 184.

121–122. *His semblable . . . nothing more.* His

only equal is in his mirror, and those who imitate him are merely his shadows. *Trace*, follow.

152. *Hangers*, " straps by which the rapier hung from the girdle, often richly ornamented."

169. *Laid on twelve for nine.* The meaning is not certain, but probably " the King wagers that Laertes —famous as a fencer and therefore able to afford his rival odds—will not have made his twelve hits until Hamlet's hits are nine ; if Hamlet falls short of nine, Laertes wins."

188. *This lapwing . . . head.* The lapwing was said to do this as soon as hatched, and was also a symbol of insincerity. Hamlet implies that Osric is a forward, conceited, insincere youngster.

193. *A kind of yesty collection . . . winnowed opinions.* This difficult passage has been much discussed and emended. Dr. Johnson offers a good explanation : " These men have got the cant of the day, a superficial readiness of slight and cursory conversation, a kind of frothy collection of fashionable prattle which yet carries them through the most select and approving judgments. This airy facility of talk sometimes imposes upon wise men." " Fond " is often emended to " fann'd," which goes well with " winnowed."

226–227. *Since no man has aught . . . betimes ?* " If we possess nothing except our personality, what matters it to leave the adventitious things of life soon or late ? " (Dowden). Another much-disputed passage.

249–253. *But in my terms of honour . . . my name ungored.* " But I cannot be formally reconciled to you until experts in the code of honour assure me, supporting their opinion by precedents, that I can do so without damage to my reputation."

291. *Fat.* Some editors, repelled by this word, have suggested emendations such as " faint " and " hot." There is a tradition that Hamlet was played

by Richard Burbage, a great tragic actor and a friend of Shakespeare's, and that the line was appropriate to him. Some editors suggest that this line and the "thirty years" of Act V., Scene i., line 172, were added merely to make the part suit Burbage. But whether "fat" means obese or simply out of training it may be defended as applicable to Hamlet.

Laertes wounds Hamlet, etc. In the First Quarto the stage direction is: "They catch one anothers Rapiers, and both are wounded, Laertes falles downe, the Queene falls downe and dies." In the First Folio: "In scuffling they change Rapiers."

An expert fencer would have no great difficulty in disarming his opponent, by striking the rapier out of his hand, or by closing and wresting it from him.

Does Hamlet realize that there is treachery immediately he is wounded ?

309. *Woodcock.* This bird was often used as a decoy.

329. *Is thy union here ?* Shakespeare can never resist a pun or a quibble, however tragic the occasion. Does the ferocity of this pun justify it ?

368. *This quarry cries on havoc,* This heap of dead bodies calls for merciless slaughter (in revenge). Or ; This heap of dead bodies suggests a fight in which no quarter has been given. *Havoc* = "No quarter ! "

HELPS TO FURTHER STUDY

I.—THE TEXT OF SHAKESPEARE'S PLAYS

§ I

NOWADAYS, when a play or any other book is to be published, the author sends a carefully-prepared manuscript to the printer, and as soon as the type has been set up he receives proofs, which he revises and corrects to make sure that there shall be no mistakes in the book. So when we buy, say, a volume of plays by Mr. Bernard Shaw, we know that we have exactly what he wrote. But we cannot feel any such complete certainty with regard to a play of Shakespeare's. The modern science of bibliography, which deals with the methods of printers and booksellers, has made it clear that Elizabethan books were usually published without any proof-correction by the authors, and that Shakespeare's plays were often printed from manuscripts which were anything but carefully prepared.

In Elizabethan times the modern ideas of authorship and copyright hardly existed. When a dramatist had written a play he sold the manuscript to a company of actors ; the various parts and cues were copied so that the players could learn them ; and the original was handed to the prompter. During rehearsal and performance stage directions were added, with occasional notes about properties and so forth, lines and even whole scenes were crossed out or scribbled in, and the manuscript suffered from hard wear and tear. (Any amateur actor or producer will appreciate all this !) Sometimes the revisions were extensive. Marlowe's *Doctor Faustus*, for example, appears to have been revised at intervals for a number of years by the simple process of tearing out a few more pages of poetry and adding another scene of crude farce. Shakespeare's *Macbeth*, to mention only one instance, contains some witch-scenes added by another writer, and Shakespeare himself began his career by touching up old plays for revival. At the best the manuscript would suffer a good deal ; at the worst the total effect must have been disastrous, and it is not likely that fair copies were often made, for this cost money and increased the danger of the play being stolen.

§ 2.

We have considered the fortunes of the playhouse manuscript. We have to consider now the printed play, the quarto book for which the Elizabethan reader paid fivepence or sixpence at the bookseller's shop, in St. Paul's Churchyard perhaps, and which he took home to be read—and perhaps to be preserved, that collectors might bid hundreds of pounds for it at a twentieth-century auction. Modern scholars have shown us something of the process by which the manuscript became the printed book, and while the compositor stands fingering his type and glowering—as well he may—at the " copy " in front of him, we can peep over his shoulder and glimpse the " copy " ourselves.

If the publisher was an honest man that " copy " was bought from the actors, who sold it because a " pirated " version had already appeared without their consent, or because they were short of money— their theatre being closed on account of the plague, perhaps, or their audiences having deserted them for some counter-attraction. In this case the compositor's "copy" was the playhouse prompt-book which has been described, often in the dramatist's handwriting, and with all its imperfections on its head. Fourteen of Shakespeare's plays were published thus, and are known as the "good quartos."

But not all publishers were honest; some were "pirates," who cared nothing for ownership or accuracy so long as they could sell a book which met the public demand for copies of a successful play. If they could get an actor to steal the playhouse manuscript the version issued would be fairly accurate, but more frequently our compositor would find himself struggling with copy much less reliable than that already described. A player who had had a part in the play would write down his own lines and what he could remember of the rest; or a shorthand-writer would be sent to sit in the darkest corner of one of the galleries and to take down as much as he could of the play while it was being performed; and either method might produce a version which was little more than a burlesque of the original, with many mistakes and omissions.* Five plays of Shakespeare's, now known as the "bad quartos," were "pirated" thus during his lifetime.

Whatever the origin of the "copy" before him, the compositor's methods and problems were the same. Occasionally, no doubt, he had a good, plain manuscript. More often he had one which, wholly or in part, was very difficult to read. He misunderstood the writer sometimes, he made mistakes of his

---

* " Some of my plaies haue (vnknown to me, and without any of my direction) accidentally come into the Printer's handes, and therefore so corrupt and mangled (copied onely by the eare) that I haue beene as vnable to know them, as ashamde to chalenge them."—Thomas Heywood, 1608. And see A. W. Pollard : *Shakespeare's Fight with the Pirates* (Cambridge University Press, 7s. 6d.).

own, and sometimes too he would "improve" the original in sense or spelling or punctuation, not always to its advantage. And no matter how many mistakes or alterations were made, the author rarely had an opportunity of correcting them.

§ 3.

When we turn from the quartos, good and bad, to the famous "First Folio," it looks at first sight as though this would be a great improvement. It is a collected edition which appeared in 1623, seven years after Shakespeare's death, a large volume of nearly a thousand pages in double column, and for most of the plays the chief or only authority. It contains all the plays that are now usually ascribed to Shakespeare (except *Pericles*, which is his only in part), and includes twenty not previously published. It was edited by the poet's friends and fellow-actors, John Heminges and Henry Condell, who claimed that they had used his own "papers" and printed his work "according to the true original copies." If this were really true, if the editing had been carefully done, Shakespearean scholars would have been spared enormous labour ; but on examination it is only too plain that the First Folio was printed from earlier quartos and from playhouse manuscripts, so that it "went to press" under much the same conditions as the "good quartos" and has no higher authority.

§ 4.

It need not be doubted, however, that in the First Folio we have the great bulk of Shakespeare's dramatic work, presented with substantial accuracy. This will be plain at once if the Folio is compared with the *Globe Shakespeare*, the standard text, which the present edition follows. But it will be equally plain that there are innumerable differences in detail, some of them very important, and mistakes and obscurities abound. A comparison of the First Folio with the quartos reveals, moreover, that some plays exist in different versions, with nothing except internal evidence to show that one has more authority than another.

The effort to clear up these difficulties, to get closer to what Shakespeare wrote and to make his plays more easily readable for us, has occupied the energy and ingenuity of a host of critics. Nicholas Rowe, the dramatist, began the work in his edition of 1709. He divided up the plays into acts and scenes (sometimes not very wisely), added locations of the scenes, many stage directions, and the lists of the characters, and made some verbal corrections. These emendations were at first largely guess-work, and though some of them were brilliant, on the whole the effect was bad, because the aim was rather to " improve " the text according to the editor's taste, than to find out what Shakespeare actually wrote. But purely arbitrary methods were slowly abandoned. Throughout the eighteenth and nineteenth centuries there was steady advance in the comparison of the oldest texts available and the study of vocabulary and phrasing in Shakespeare's work and in Elizabethan literature generally. This patient labour by generations of able critics culminated in the *Cambridge Shakespeare*, edited by W. G. Clark and W. Aldis Wright in 1863–66, of which the *Globe Shakespeare* is a slightly revised edition in one volume. This is the best complete text we possess, though it is certainly not perfect.

In the present century great advances have been made by the invention of new methods, more effective and more scientific. Critics used to be oppressed by the belief that a play might have been copied and recopied many times, with the probability of fresh mistakes every time, before it came to the printer. Modern bibliographical criticism has shown us that, as explained above, it was usually the author's manuscript which the compositor had before him, and nowadays when we peep over his shoulder it is Shakespeare's own handwriting which we glimpse.

And at last we know what that writing was like. The dramatist's six extant signatures are of little help in themselves, but modern palæographical criticism, proceeding with a minute exactness which Sherlock Holmes might envy, has shown that one of the additions to the Elizabethan play of *Sir Thomas More* * is almost certainly Shakespeare's composition in his own handwriting. If it is not his, then it is very like his. He wrote in the old English style he had learned at Stratford Grammar School, very different from the Italian style which we all use now and which was then coming into fashion. His carelessness made it easy for the compositor to confuse some of his letters or groups of letters—" e " and " d," for example, or " oi " and " or." So the editor of to-day who is puzzled by some problem in the text writes down the doubtful words in Shakespeare's own handwriting, and can see what mistakes the compositor would be most likely to make.

This new method has been reinforced by others, such as the study of peculiar spellings and of the punctuation of the early editions, for it has been shown that the dramatist used capital letters and stops and brackets, not to indicate the grammatical structure of the sentence as we do, but to guide the actor in pauses, intonations, and stage-business. These methods give very interesting results, and are

* *The Book of Sir Thomas More*, a manuscript play now in the British Museum, most probably by Anthony Munday. When it was submitted to the Queen's Master of the Revels, to be licensed for performance, he censored a number of passages because they dealt with political matters. The necessary alterations and additions were made by five different writers, Shakespeare being one, and apparently it was not acted after all.

being applied in the *New Cambridge Shakespeare* which Sir Arthur Quiller-Couch and Mr. J. Dover Wilson are now editing. An excellent introduction to modern textual criticism is provided by the preface to *The Tempest* in the *New Cambridge Shakespeare*, together with the essay (in the *Review of English Studies*, April 1925) by Sir Edmund K. Chambers on " The Integrity of *The Tempest*."

II.—THE TEXT AND DATE OF "HAMLET"

Although there is no doubt that we possess *Hamlet* substantially as Shakespeare wrote it, the text of the play presents many tantalizing problems, and so does the attempt to decide the date of composition.

It is quite plain that a play or plays about *Hamlet* were staged long before the first printed version appeared in 1603. The earliest known reference is in Thomas Nashe's preface to Greene's *Menaphon*, 1589 ; he inveighs against a writer who has left " the trade of Nouerint " (*i.e.* lawyer's clerk) to " runne through euery Art " and " affoord you whole Hamlets, I should say handfulls of Tragicall speeches." This may refer to Shakespeare or to Thomas Kyd, author of *The Spanish Tragedy* (see page 174, below) : Kyd seems the more likely. There are later references by Henslowe the theatre-manager in 1594 ; by Thomas Lodge in 1596 ; by Gabriel Hervey in 1598 (or 1600 ?) ; and by Dekker in 1602. This Hamlet play may have been written by Kyd or Shakespeare or both ; or there may have been more than one play. Of the references mentioned, only Hervey's assigns the play to Shakespeare, and here the date is uncertain. *Hamlet* is not included in the famous list of Shakespeare's plays given by Francis Meres in his *Palladis Tamia* (Wits Treasury) in 1598 ; but it can be argued that this list was not meant to be complete, or that the old play had been revised by Shakespeare without his name being connected with it. We know that he revised a number of plays, and that revision and collaboration were very common in Elizabethan drama. At least it is certain that there was an old play (sometimes called the " Ur-Hamlet ") and that it was acted by the Lord Chamberlain's company, to which Shakespeare belonged.

Under the date July 26, 1602, there appears an entry in the Stationers' Register of a book about to be published—" A booke called *' the Revenge of* HAMLETT *Prince [of] Denmarke' as yt was latelie acted by the Lord Chamberlayne his servants.* vjd." This was entered to James Roberts, a friend of Shakespeare's company, who printed all their playbills, and by the rules of the Stationers' Company the entry precluded any other bookseller from publishing the play. It indicates that authorized publication had already been decided upon, perhaps because the piracy had been discovered. But as there is no existing edition which can be dated earlier than May 1603 (First Quarto), the attempt to prevent or forestall the pirated version was a failure. Shakespeare's company may have been too occupied with other things in 1603, for in that year they were transferred to the patronage of James I., as the " King's Men," on the death of Elizabeth ; and plague in London compelled them to spend some time touring the provinces. Whatever the explanation, the first edition of *Hamlet* was obviously pirated. It is known as

The First Quarto.   (Q₁).   1603.

' The Tragicall Historie of Hamlet Prince of Denmarke By William Shakespeare As it hath beene diuerse times acted by his Highnesse seruants in the Cittie of London : as also in the two Vniversities of Cambridge and Oxford, and else-where [*Device*] At London printed for N. L. and Iohn Trundell. 1603."

This is obviously the product of dishonest methods, for it is very much mutilated. Internal evidence indicates (not quite certainly) that the play was taken down in shorthand during performance ; except for the parts of Marcellus and Voltimand, which are so accurate that they seem to have been copied from a player's script, or dictated by the player. The first two acts are so much nearer the authorized version than the rest that it has been suggested that the thief obtained access to the playhouse manuscript, but was detected when he had got to the end of Act II. That Shakespeare and his company resented the piracy and tried to check it is clear from the next edition.

Q_1 contains 2,143 lines—more than 1,500 lines less than Q_2. It gives substantially the whole *action* of the play as it appears in Q_2, but there are many differences in dialogue, etc. Polonius is " Corambis," Reynaldo " Montano," Osric " a Bragart Gentleman," and Francisco " First Centinel." Lines and scenes are transposed. Yorick's skull has been only twelve years in the ground. It is the King, not Laertes, who suggests poisoning the rapier. The Queen promises to help Hamlet against the King and is in league with Horatio. The contemplative element in Hamlet is much less developed, and his madness more prominent. The Player King has some good lines which are not in Q_2 or F_1, but many of the finest poetical and philosophical passages of the later play do not appear, or are so corrupted that they read almost like burlesque. The first two acts correspond more closely with Q_2 than the rest of the play.

Extracts from Q_1 are given on pages 203–206, below.

The Second Quarto. (Q_2). 1604.

" The Tragicall Historie of Hamlet, Prince of Denmarke. By William Shakespeare. Newly imprinted and enlarged to almost as much againe as it was, according to the true and perfect Coppie. [*Device*] At London. Printed by I. R. for N. L. and are to be sold at his shoppe vnder Saint Dunstons Church in Fleetstreet. 1604." (See the frontispiece of the present edition.)

Q_2 is carelessly printed and punctuated, but its publication was almost certainly arranged by Shakespeare himself, probably from the playhouse manuscript. This edition contains 3,719 lines, and the difference represents an extraordinary superiority over Q_1 in intellectual and poetic power. This is substantially the *Hamlet* we know, lacking about 80 or 90 lines of the text which is now generally accepted.

Three more quarto editions appeared before Shakespeare's death—evidence of the play's popularity—and these all reprint Q_2 with a few additional errors.

The First Folio. (F_1). 1623.

" The Tragedie of Hamlet " occupies pages 152–280. This was evidently not printed from the same manuscript as Q_2, being an abridgment for acting purposes which contains 80 to 90 lines not in Q_2, but omits 218 lines there given, and has many minor differences. In general it is " more theatrical, but less literary, than the text of 1604," and it almost certainly represents the revisions which had been made—some of them perhaps by Shakespeare himself—for revivals between 1604 and 1623. There are some notable omissions, especially the greater part of Act IV., Scene iv., including Hamlet's soliloquy.

As far as *Hamlet* was concerned, later Folios were merely reprints of the first, with minor corrections and mistakes.

The *Hamlet* of the *Globe Shakespeare*, which is followed in this edition, is a combination of the Q_2 and F_1 texts, emended and much modernized, with many stage directions and scene headings added.

HELPS TO FURTHER STUDY

The problems presented by these texts may never be finally solved. The most expert critics disagree, and there are three main theories :

1. Q_1 is a bad version of an old Hamlet play, *not by Shakespeare*, which he had partly re-written—about as far as the end of Act II., and in some other passages. Shakespeare's *Hamlet* makes its first appearance in Q_2.
2. Q_1 is a bad version of an early play by Shakespeare—his first draft of the tragedy.
3. Q_1 is a bad version of the play, by Shakespeare, which was published in Q_2 ; all the differences are due to mistakes.

It will now be clear that the problem of the date of composition cannot be considered apart from the textual problems. It is possible that Shakespeare wrote a part or the whole of a Hamlet play before 1589. It is certain, by comparison with his early work, that at that time he could not have written the *Hamlet* of Q_2 and F_1. The composition of this last play is generally assigned to 1600–1601. The later time-limit is fixed as July 1602, by the entry in the Stationers' Register ; and the earlier time-limit is probably fixed as 1598, by the omission of *Hamlet* from the list, already mentioned, in Francis Meres' *Palladis Tamia*. A number of small points seem to indicate that *Hamlet* was written soon after *Julius Cæsar* (1599) : the revenge theme, the treatment of the supernatural element, the resemblance between Brutus and Hamlet and the references to Cæsar in the later tragedy. With the internal evidence of style, metre, and diction this indicates 1600–1601 as the most probable date.

III.—THE SOURCE OF THE PLAY

It was the accepted custom for Elizabethan dramatists to base their plays on stories or ballads or older plays, and if these were already familiar to the audience they were apparently all the more welcome in their new form. Shakespeare was typical of his time in this as in so many other things; "sources" have been discovered for nearly all his plays.

In the case of *Hamlet*, however, there are uncertainties and conflicting theories. The story of Hamlet seems to have developed from ancient Icelandic and Scandinavian legends; its earliest known appearance is in the Latin *Historiæ Danicæ* (History of the Danes) written by Saxo Grammaticus about the beginning of the thirteenth century, and printed in 1514. It is there a primitive and brutal story of murder, feigned insanity, and bloodthirsty revenge.

In 1570 it was translated into French by Francis de Belleforest in the fifth volume of his *Histoires Tragiques*.

An English version of Belleforest appeared under the title of *The Hystorie of Hamblet*, and this is regarded by some critics as the source of Shakespeare's tragedy. But there is one difficulty. The only existing copy of *The Hystorie of Hamblet* is dated 1608—some years after the play—and it has not been proved that the book had been published earlier, while the resemblances between the two are not absolutely conclusive because they are too general. Moreover, it is quite probable that the translation of the "Hystorie" was prompted by the success of Shakespeare's play.

Another possible source is suggested by an old German play of which only one manuscript copy exists : *Der Bestrafte Brudermord, oder Prinz Hamlet aus Dænnemark* (" Fratricide Punished, or Prince Hamlet of Denmark ").

Internal evidence shows that this is most probably a translation of an English play ; a number of Elizabethan companies acted in Germany, and some of their plays were translated. The English original must have been very crude—and this brings us back to the old Hamlet play, by Kyd or another, which has been mentioned already and which seems the most probable source of Shakespeare's play. It is particularly noteworthy that the character who appears as Polonius in Q_2 and F_1 is called Corambis in Q_1 and Corambus in the German play.

But we must remember that as literature all these " sources " are worthless. Shakespeare's masterpiece owes far more to his own genius than to anything else, and his indebtedness is trivial when compared with his wonderful transmutation of the raw material of his plays.

IV.—THE REVENGE PLAYS AND " HAMLET "

A play of Shakespeare's, like any other work of art, may be studied as a thing complete in itself, isolated, and needing no historical setting. But we can appreciate his work all the more fully if we know something of the conditions under which it was written.

When he was a young man he came to London penniless, and throughout his career he was dependent for a livelihood upon his earnings as an actor and a dramatist, and, to a much greater extent, upon his profits as a shareholder in the Globe Theatre and (later) the Blackfriars " Private " Theatre. This meant that he had constantly to study the needs and possibilities of these theatres, especially the Globe. He wrote his plays to be acted in daylight upon a small stage which had no scenery, or very little, and simple "properties." He had to depend for his effects entirely upon the power of the actor and the spoken word to sway the imagination of the auditors, but these were so close to the stage, in so intimate an emotional relationship with the actor, that we need hardly commiserate Shakespeare upon the poverty of his theatrical resources. The Globe Theatre had a very motley audience, ranging from the illiterate "groundlings" who stood in the pit to fastidious courtiers and critics who sat in the galleries. They wanted, in the main, poetry, bloodshed, horseplay, pageantry, and variegated action, all of which Shakespeare gave them so effectively that he became the most successful playwright of the time as well as the greatest of poets and dramatists.

The taste of the audience was liable to changes of fashion, and these had to be catered for. When a Jew was hanged at Tyburn in 1594, with a mob howling curses at him for having tried to poison Queen Elizabeth, anti-Jewish plays suddenly became the vogue, and another company drew crowds with a revival of Christopher Marlowe's tragedy, *The Jew of Malta*. Shakespeare was called upon to produce a play with a Jew as the villain, and being a popular playwright with his living to earn he wrote *The Merchant of Venice*. But because he was also a great dramatist his play has kept the stage for three hundred years after the anti-Jewish plays have been forgotten, and his Jew is portrayed with unprecedented power and sympathy.

Hamlet is a much greater example of a similar process—the creation of a masterpiece prompted by a transient popular demand. It was one of Shakespeare's forerunners, Thomas Kyd, who gave the revenge play its tremendous vogue, by the success of *The Spanish Tragedy* about 1589. This was one of the most popular dramas of the time, and as late as 1602 "adicyons" were being written for it by Ben

Jonson, while it is mentioned in contemporary writings more often than any other play. It is dull enough reading to-day, but we can recognize at once the typical ingredients of the revenge play—the ghost, the suicides and murders, and the play within the play. It is obviously indebted for much of its machinery and atmosphere to the tragedies of Seneca, who had greater influence upon Elizabethan drama than any other classical dramatist. But it must be given credit for a theatrical effectiveness and an attempt at subtlety in characterization which mark a definite advance in technical power.

The fashion thus set continued into the early years of the seventeenth century, the revenge play merging into the decadent tragedy of horror, and Chapman, Marston, and Webster were among the writers who contributed to it.

Whether it was Shakespeare or Kyd who wrote the first *Hamlet*, it was Shakespeare who gave it final form and used the hackneyed devices of the revenge play to create a masterpiece of poetic tragedy. For him it had a double importance : it was not only his most popular success, but the first of his great tragedies, and it is these tragedies, *Hamlet, Othello, Macbeth,* and *King Lear,* with his last lovely comedy, *The Tempest,* which set the seal upon his greatness. His earlier work culminated in *Henry IV., Parts I. and II., Twelfth Night,* and *Julius Cæsar,* all of them showing an easy mastery and an even balance between thought and style, and it is possible that Shakespeare might have stopped short at their limited perfection, a great dramatist but not a supreme poet and interpreter of human life. Then something happened to Shakespeare himself. Outwardly his life went on more prosperously than ever, but it seems plain that some great crisis in his inner life, some profound and tragic spiritual experience, is reflected in the series of tragic plays. The easy mastery disappeared : he wrote with a new passionate intensity of thought and feeling, so that his later work is sometimes obscure and broken from the pressure of ideas upon the inadequate instrument of speech. As a man and an artist he struggled forward, making ever greater demands upon the dramatic form which was his means of expression, and so continuing that development which has gone on in drama since the days of the ancient Greeks—a development from external to internal conflict. In *Hamlet* it is revelation of character, of what men think and feel, of the struggles in their own hearts, that counts for more than what they do : a criticism of life has come to be of greater dramatic interest and power than plot and counterplot or the clash of sword on shield. *Hamlet* was Shakespeare's triumphant demonstration that it was possible to write a play which was a successful stage entertainment for a popular audience, and at the same time the expression of a great poet's vision of the eternal wonder and mystery of human life.

ON THINKING IT OVER

" Hamlet is a name ; his speeches and sayings but the idle coinage of the poet's brain. What then, are they not real ? They are as real as our own thoughts. Their reality is in the reader's mind. It is *we* who are Hamlet."
WILLIAM HAZLITT.

" It is easy to theorise about *Hamlet*—especially if we ignore the text." G. F. BRADBY.

THE modern reader of Shakespeare is indebted to generations of editors and critics, who have laboured to present a good text of the plays and to explain difficult words and phrases. In so far as their work helps us to appreciate Shakespeare more fully, it is of the greatest value, but in itself it is remote from Shakespeare's purpose. When all this business of notes and explanations is done, one all-important thing remains : *Hamlet* is neither a collection of problems, nor material for examination-papers, nor a kind of fancy-dress party with a gory conclusion. It is a tragic play about living men and women, terribly real and true, written to be acted for our interest and—in the highest sense—our enjoyment. If we do not enjoy *Hamlet* we know nothing about it, and no laborious lumbering of our memories with editorial matter and ready-made critical opinions can make good our loss. Notes and criticisms are worthless except in so far as they lead us to appreciate the tragedy as a great living work of art, to be enjoyed

as we enjoy a play by Shaw or Galsworthy or Barrie.*
Nothing less than this is of any value to us, and having
reached this—no very difficult matter—we find that
every time we read the play again or see it acted with
intelligence there is something fresh to be enjoyed,
some touch of beauty or wisdom which we have before
passed over unobserved.

Every one who cares for Shakespeare's plays should
try to see them acted, though there are more bad
performances than good ones. Perhaps a good repertory company gives the best rendering of all : the
plays were originally written to be acted by a good
repertory company. Performances by touring companies are sometimes astonishingly bad, partly because none of the players can speak blank verse, and
in these days of the great renaissance of community
drama an amateur production is often to be preferred,
when sincerity and enthusiasm and imagination
counterbalance the inevitable deficiencies in technique. For the actors and producer, at least, the
amateur production is as profitable as it is enjoyable.
We can learn to appreciate Shakespeare's plays, as
plays, in the theatre more than anywhere else, especially when acting in them is preceded and accompanied by thoughtful study. But the supreme magic
of their poetry is probably heard best of all in our
private re-reading, for then we can give the lines the
ideal music of the imagination.

When we are watching a performance of *Hamlet* we
are not troubled by any problems, but as soon as we
begin to think it over we find ourselves asking questions about the characters. Many of them are
questions to which no final answers can ever be given,
and that helps to explain why they have fascinated so
many people. Some are insoluble because of inconsistencies in the play itself : when he wrote *Hamlet*

* If you have read no plays by these writers you should look for
them in your school library without delay.

Shakespeare had not attained that mastery of tragic drama which he shows in *Macbeth* and *Othello* ; he was feeling his way. Moreover, he was working on an old play or story whose chief incidents were so well known that he would not alter them, and some of these incidents may have remained, in conflict with his own conception of the play and its hero. But most of the insoluble problems deal with human motives and character, which we can, and do, discuss for ever.

1. Why was Hamlet so long in killing the King ? Why did he not " sweep to his revenge " after his interview with the Ghost, instead of waiting in misery for months and bringing so many innocent people, himself included, to destruction ?

Many different explanations have been offered, among them the following :

That external obstacles prevented him.

(You can soon refute this if you study the play.)

That Hamlet could kill a man on impulse, but not deliberately in cold blood.

That he had conscientious scruples.

That too much thought had made him incapable of action.

That he was afraid.

That he was sunk in a deep melancholy and disgust with life which made decided action impossible.

Say what you think of these opinions, and give your own ; and remember that your statements must be supported by quotations or direct references to the play if they are to be of any value.

Read Sections 2–6 before writing about this.

2. Another question much disputed is whether Hamlet was mad. The Hamlet of the legend and the old play undoubtedly feigned madness to protect himself from the King—as Lucius Junius Brutus did, and David when he was in the hands of the Philistines.

HAMLET

Was Hamlet sane throughout the play, and sometimes pretending to be mad? If so, why did he pretend, when it would have been safer still to behave quite normally?—Or was he sometimes mad and sometimes merely pretending?—Or was he never mad, but driven to the verge of madness?

3. As the chief features of Hamlet's character Dr. A. C. Bradley notes: (1) an inclination " to nervous instability, to rapid and extreme changes of feeling and mood," the feelings of the moment absorbing him; (2) an exquisite moral sensibility, with " an unbounded delight and faith in everything good and beautiful "; " a disposition to idealise " [Laertes, for instance] and a horror of evil; (3) intellectual genius, which makes him different from all those about him and from most of Shakespeare's heroes. This genius " shows itself, fitfully, in the affairs of life, as unusual quickness of perception, great agility in shifting the mental attitude, a striking rapidity and fertility in resource; so that, when his natural belief in others does not make him unwary, Hamlet easily sees through them and masters them, and no one can be much less like the typical helpless dreamer. It shows itself in conversation chiefly in the form of wit or humour . . . and . . . imagination."

Say what you think of this, and remember that you must not accept any detail unless you can support it by evidence from the play.

4. It is generally believed that when this play was written Shakespeare's own life was darkened by some terrible tragedy, and that in shaping Hamlet, whom he endowed with his own great powers, he poured out his mental agony and his dark questionings of the universe.

Was Hamlet his normal self in the play? If not, what was he like before his father's death?

5. Mr. G. F. Bradby points out that Horatio presents two different and irreconcilable characters:

ON THINKING IT OVER

(1) Horatio is a trusted confidant of Marcellus and Bernardo (Act I., Scenes i. and ii.) ; who knows more about Danish politics than they do (I. i.) ; knew Hamlet's father well (I., i. and ii.), and saw him fight " the ambitious Norway," in the year of Hamlet's birth (I. i. and V. i.), so that he must be much older than Hamlet ; and he is Hamlet's intimate friend of long standing (III. ii.). He came to Elsinore to attend the late King's funeral, and has therefore been there about two months when the play begins.

(2) The " second Horatio " Hamlet apparently meets with surprise in Act I., Scene ii., inquiring what has brought him from Wittenberg ; he is ignorant of Danish customs (I. iv.) ; saw the late King *once* (I. ii.) ; has never heard of Yorick, and does not know Osric or Laertes (V., i. and ii.).

There are a number of other small points not catalogued above. It looks as though Shakespeare changed his mind about Horatio and interpolated passages without completely revising the character. Do you agree ?

6. It is possible that there are two Hamlets to be found in the play as well as two Horatios—that some incongruous characteristics of Hamlet survive from the old play, or that others represent Shakespeare's second thoughts about him, added without adequate revision. Consider especially Hamlet's treatment of Ophelia and of Polonius' dead body ; his behaviour on the voyage to England, and his later references to Rosencrantz and Guildenstern ; his quarrel with Laertes, and his transparently insincere apology. Can these points be reconciled with the rest of his character, the thinker and poet of Shakespeare's creation ; or are they merely survivals of the old half-barbarous Hamlet ? Critics are divided on this question : you should form your own opinion from study of the play, searching carefully for such points as that mentioned in Section 37 below.

7. "We perceive that Laertes takes after his father, and that the males of this family are addicted to long-windedness ; and surmise that Lady Polonius (as I must call her) has died of it some while before. From the first we have a sense of the most pathetic orphaned loneliness about Ophelia. Throughout she has no one to turn to, no woman to give her advice. . . . Her brother is no sooner gone than her father turns on her and reads her another lecture—reams of worldly counsel, all withered, conventional."—Sir A. T. Quiller-Couch.

The " Mad Scene, if one looks at it with a cold eye, is really very poor. It depends entirely for its effect upon poor wispy Ophelia. The cardboard King and Queen are of course only lookers-on. They don't care a halfpenny. . . . And who can believe that a solitary violet withered when that silly fussy old pomposity died ? And who can believe that Ophelia really loved him, and wasn't thankful to think how peaceful breakfast would be without his preaching ? "—Katherine Mansfield.

" Of [Ophelia's] subsequent madness, what can be said ? What an affecting, what an astonishing, picture of a mind utterly, hopelessly wrecked ! past hope, past care. . . . Her wild, rambling fancies ; her aimless, broken speeches ; her quick transitions from gaiety to sadness . . . all are so true to the life, that we forget to wonder, and can only weep."—Mrs. Jameson.

" Ophelia is a character almost too exquisitely touching to be dwelt upon."—William Hazlitt.

" Ophelia is a doll without intellect."—John Masefield.

Say what you think of these criticisms, and give your own estimate of the character of Ophelia.

8. Hamlet's treatment of Ophelia needs discussion. " I loved Ophelia," he cries over her grave ; but he told her brutally, " I loved you not." Which is

true ? Is he the kind of man to play with her, as Laertes and Polonius suggest ? Does he despise her weakness ? Has his mother's conduct filled him with disgust and loathing for all women ? In Act III., Scene i., does he discover that Ophelia is acting as a decoy; and if so, does this excuse his cruel treatment of her in that scene ?

"If the story had been only the story of Hamlet and Ophelia we should have felt that Hamlet richly deserved his fate at the hands of Laertes."—G. F. Bradby. Do you agree ?

9. The King is perhaps more interesting when one thinks over the play than while it is in progress. In murdering his brother, marrying the Queen, and securing the throne he seems to have shown himself a ruthless, bold, and determined criminal. Does he appear in this character during the play ? Or do you agree with Mr. Bradby that Shakespeare has deliberately toned him down, making him " treacherous but rather tame," because his " tameness makes it harder for Hamlet to kill him " ?

10. Write a paragraph comparing the King with Macbeth.

11. To what extent is the Queen guilty ? You must examine carefully all the evidence in the play before you answer.

12. In the First Quarto the Queen swears that she never knew of the murder, promises to help Hamlet, and is Horatio's trusted companion. Is the accepted version of the play an improvement, on these points ?

13. "The Queen his mother Lives almost by his looks," says the King (page 114), when speaking of Hamlet. Is this true ? And is Hamlet fond of his mother ? If so, how does it help to explain his state of mind when the play opens ?

14. Is the Queen fond of Ophelia ? If so, does this tell us anything about the Queen's rather vaguely drawn character ?

15. On the stage Polonius is often made the comic character of the play, a completely foolish and ridiculous old man. Do you think this is the right interpretation of the part?

16. Polonius says of himself:

> " By heaven, it is as proper to our age
> To cast beyond ourselves in our opinions
> As it is common for the younger sort
> To lack discretion."

Is this self-estimate correct?

17. What can be said in defence of Laertes?

18. Apparently Shakespeare intended the sub-plot of Laertes' revenge to enforce the main plot by its handling of a similar theme in a different manner: does this succeed? Does this relationship of plot and sub-plot show any resemblance to *King Lear*?

19. Is Horatio of any help to Hamlet? If so, in what way?

20. Do you think that the Ghost is meant to be objective in Act I. and subjective in Act III., Scene iv.? Does Hamlet behave differently to the Ghost on the two occasions?

21. There is a tradition that Shakespeare himself took the part of the Ghost. It is not an easy part to play well, and a number of good actors have chosen it. What is your own opinion as to the way in which the Ghost should speak his lines?

22. Do you think that Hamlet, before the play-scene, really doubts the honesty of the Ghost?

23. How would the play lose or gain if the Ghost were omitted and Hamlet learned of the murder by some natural method?

24. " Perhaps the vitalizing power of Shakespeare is best seen in the loving care that he sometimes spends on subsidiary characters, whose connection with the plot is but slight. The young Osric, in *Hamlet*, has no business in the play except to carry Laertes' chal-

lenge to Hamlet. Shakespeare draws his portrait; we learn that he is a landowner, and perceive that he is an accomplished courtier. Hamlet and Horatio discuss him at some length, and his own speech shows how seriously he is preoccupied with all the etiquette and formality of Court life. He exists, it cannot be doubted, merely as a foil for Hamlet's wit and melancholy. When the mind is wholly taken up with tragic issues, when it is brooding on a great sorrow, or foreboding a hopeless event, the little daily affairs of life continue unaltered: tables are served, courtesies interchanged, and the wheels of society revolve at their accustomed pace. Osric is the representative of society; his talk is of gentility, skill in fencing, and the elegance of the proffered wager. How distant and dream-like it all seems to Hamlet, and to those who are in his secret! But this trivial society is real and necessary, strong with the giant strength of custom and institution. Shakespeare demonstrates its reality by showing us a live inhabitant. He might have entrusted the challenge to a walking gentleman, and concluded the business in a few lines. By making a scene of it, he adds a last touch of pathos to the loneliness of Hamlet, and gives a last opportunity for the display of that incomparable vein of irony."—Sir Walter Raleigh: *Shakespeare*.

On the model of this write a paragraph about another minor character or incident in the play.

25. "The society of the Danish Court is created with Shakespeare's fullest power. It is not an image of the world in little, like the world of the late historical plays. It is an image of the world as intellect is made to feel it. It is a society governed by the enemies of intellect, by the sensual and the worldly, by deadly sinners and the philosophers of bread and cheese. The King is a drunken, incestuous murderer, who fears intellect. The Queen is a false woman, who cannot understand intellect. Polonius is a counsellor

who suspects intellect. Ophelia is a doll without intellect. Laertes is a boor who destroys intellect. The courtiers are parasites who flourish on the decay of intellect. Fortinbras, bright and noble, marching to the drum to win a dunghill, gives a colour to the folly. The only friends of the wise man are Horatio, the schoolfellow, and the leader of a cry of players."
—John Masefield : *Shakespeare*.

Is this a fair estimate ?

26. *Hamlet* is by far Shakespeare's longest play, and Hamlet's own part is also exceptionally long. The editors of the *New Hudson Shakespeare* have calculated that the numbers of lines spoken by the chief characters are as follows : King, 544 ; Hamlet, 1,458 ; Polonius, 350 ; Horatio, 284 ; Laertes, 202 ; Rosencrantz, 101 ; Guildenstern, 55 ; Marcellus, 68 ; First Clown, 90 ; Fortinbras, 27 ; Ghost, 95 ; Queen, 157 ; Ophelia, 158. Comment on the figures.

27. How would you explain the perennial interest of *Hamlet* (*a*) for popular audiences, (*b*) for literary critics ?

28. One of Brutus' soliloquies, in *Julius Cæsar*, Act II., Scene i., contains this passage :

" Between the acting of a dreadful thing
And the first motion, all the interim is
Like a phantasma or a hideous dream :
The Genius and the mortal instruments
Are then in council ; and the state of man,
Like to a little kingdom, suffers then
The nature of an insurrection."

Mr. Granville-Barker describes this as " a recipe for tragedy." Do you agree ? Does it apply to *Hamlet* ? What is tragedy ?

29. It has been said that in Shakespeare's tragedies " character is destiny " ; that the tragic fate of his heroes is due to some flaw in their characters (not always a vice) and a combination of circumstances in

which this flaw betrays them to destruction. Is this true of Hamlet?

30. The basic elements of drama are action, conflict, and tension. The conflict may be external, between individuals, or between groups of people; or internal, between contending emotions (such as patriotism and ambition) in an individual; or both external and internal.

Follow the conflict or conflicts in *Hamlet* through the play, and state what they are. There is a change in the external conflict at about the middle of the play.

31. Among the dramatist's most effective weapons are contrast and the heightening of suspense by a deliberate withholding of action or information. Can you find examples in *Hamlet*?

32. A play begins with the *Exposition*, or explanation, in which the characters are introduced to the audience, and the situation is explained. It proceeds through the *Complication*, in which " the plot thickens " and there is growing intensity of interest, to the *Climax*, or turning point, at which tension reaches its height. Then comes a *Resolution*, or slackening of tension, until the play reaches its *Catastrophe* or *Dénouement*, a final disentanglement of the threads of the plot that decides the fate of the principal characters and usually promises, or provides, a return to normal conditions of life.

After thinking over the action of the play as a whole, divide it into sections under the above headings. The first and most important point is to decide where the *Climax* comes: there may be one or more minor climaxes besides the major one.

33. The Exposition is always a difficult problem for a dramatist because he has to arrest the attention of his audience and, at the same time, to give them the necessary explanations without losing their interest or making them feel that information is being ladled out to them.

Is the exposition of *Hamlet* good or bad? Compare it briefly with the expositions of *As You Like It* and *The Tempest* or *Macbeth*.

34. The Dumb-show in Act III., Scene ii., has provoked a good deal of discussion, because it merely anticipates the play in dialogue. Dumb-shows were common, but were symbolical prologues, not complete anticipations.

It has been suggested (1) that Hamlet wished to make doubly sure of catching the conscience of the King by presenting the action twice; and (2) that the King was occupied with something else during the Dumb-show and did not see it at all; or (3) that his self-control endured the first representation but broke down at the second; (4) that the Dumb-show was written as an alternative to the dialogue-play, and by mistake both are preserved in the text.

Is there anything in the scene which makes one of these theories more probable than the others?

35. In "the play within the play" (pages 77–81) which lines are most probably those written and inserted by Hamlet?

36. What all-important difference in Hamlet's position is made by this "play-scene"?

37. Re-read carefully the conclusion of Act III., Scene iv. (pages 94–96; lines 157–216). Can you find anything which suggests that there are *two* endings to the scene, here incorporated in the same text by mistake?

38. In Act III., Scene iv., how does Hamlet know that he is to go to England? *Were* the letters already sealed? See the King's first speech in Scene iii., and consider whether there is any interval between this scene and the next.

39. What was Shakespeare's dramatic purpose in bringing in the humour of the graveyard scene just before the end of the tragedy?

40. A critic makes this comment on Act V., Scene ii. :

"You never suspect the errand Hamlet is on until you hear that little word, '*The interim is mine!*' It means more mischief than all the monologues! No threats, no imprecations, no more mention of smiling, damned villain; no more self-accusal; but solely and briefly '*It will be short; the interim is mine!*' Then, for the first time, we recognize the extent of the change that has been wrought in Hamlet; then, for the first time, we perfectly comprehend his quiet jesting with the Clown, his tranquil musings with Horatio. The man is transformed by a great resolve: *his mind is made up!* The return of the vessel from England will be the signal for his own execution, and therefore the moral problem is solved: the only chance of saving his life from a lawless murderer is to slay him; it has become an act of self-defence; he can do it with perfect conscience. He has calculated the return voyage; he has allowed the longest duration to his own existence and the King's. At the very moment he encounters the Clown in the churchyard he is on his death-march to the palace at Elsinore."

Criticize this in detail, with references to the play. Do not hesitate to disagree if you wish.

41. Choose a short passage from the play and comment upon it in the manner of the paragraph quoted above.

42. What dramatic purpose is served by introducing Fortinbras in the last scene?

43. "The reflections and moralizings and broodings over misfortunes inherited from Seneca, and long an essential element in the revenge plays, are also, like the sensational incidents, integrated and humanized by the conception of the hero's character. The soliloquies, though keeping to the themes and methods of contemporary drama, become landmarks in the

depiction of the inner struggle and in the general progress of the action. The absurd convention of speaking aloud one's unformed and unbidden thoughts becomes theatrically exciting, dramatically essential, and, through the reach of Shakespeare's imaginative expression, representative of the eternal battle of human frailty against the mysteries of chance and evil."—Ashley H. Thorndike : *Tragedy*.

Discuss this criticism of *Hamlet* and illustrate it by detailed references to the play.

44. Write a brief summary of each soliloquy in turn, and show how (if at all) it is a landmark in the progress of the play.

45. Do you think it is just to say that " apart from the peculiar character of the hero the play would be no more than a vulgar melodrama " ?

46. A good deal has been written about the time-scheme of *Hamlet*, although Shakespeare himself probably had no definite scheme but was content merely to give the impressions which were necessary for dramatic effect. The clearest references are Hamlet's " But two months dead " (page 22) and Ophelia's "'Tis twice two months " (page 76). One method of gaining a thorough knowledge of the play is to draw up a list of the scenes, showing when they occur and the intervals between them, based on evidence collected from the text. Special attention should be paid to the interval between Act I. and Act II., and that between Act IV., Scene iv., and Act IV., Scene v.

47. In Q_1 and Q_2 *Hamlet* is not divided into acts and scenes, and in F_1 the division stops short at Act II., Scene ii. The commonly accepted arrangement, followed in the present edition, is therefore not Shakespeare's, but his editors', and has often been adversely criticized. Suggest any alterations which you would make, and give your reasons.

48. Study the passages from Q_1 which are given in

the Appendix, and make a detailed comparison of them with the corresponding passages in this edition, pointing out any superiority of one over the other.

49. Although *Hamlet* is Shakespeare's most popular play, and it seems to bring us closer to his personality than any other, it is by no means his most nearly perfect work of art. What are its chief merits and defects and inconsistencies ?

50. One of the best ways of getting to know and love a play of Shakespeare's is to act in a full-dress performance of it, or even better perhaps, to produce it. Failing this, a great deal of enjoyment may be had from more or less impromptu form-room acting, which certainly gives players and audience an opportunity of using their imaginations in Elizabethan fashion. Another way is to imagine yourself playing *Hamlet*, say, or another leading character in one of the important scenes, and to decide exactly how you would speak your lines, what movements and gestures would be most natural and expressive, and what would be your attitude and your position with regard to the other characters at various stages of the action.

In this, as indeed in all silent reading of poetry, you should " read aloud in your mind "—hear the sound of the words as well as follow the thought—because it is impossible to appreciate all the beauty and meaning of poetry unless you hear the sound.

51. If you would rather be producer than actor, erect the stage in your mind, picture your stage-setting, and then let the play go forward. At first you may have to treat the players like puppets, showing them where to stand and when to move, but after you have had practice at this they will sometimes come to life and play out a scene without your help. This gives a new and vivid reality to the play, and is much more interesting and exciting than the cinema.

52. Hamlet's instructions to the Players (page 72)

are generally held to represent Shakespeare's opinions on acting. What are the most important points he makes? Do you think that he would be pleased with performances of his plays which you have seen?

53. What are the arguments for and against staging *Hamlet* (*a*) in the dress of to-day, (*b*) in the dress of eleventh-century Denmark? The latter period is sometimes assigned because of the reference to England's " neglected tribute " in Act III., Scene ii.

54. Make an analysis of *Hamlet* on the lines suggested in pages 171–174 of *The Teaching of English in Upper Forms*, by A. J. J. Ratcliff (Nelson's " Teaching of English " Series). The play can be treated alone, or in comparison with *Julius Cæsar*, *Macbeth*, or *Richard II*.

55. Arrange a debate on one of the following subjects :

> That Hamlet was mad.
> That Hamlet was in love with Ophelia throughout the play.
> That Polonius deserved his fate.
> That Laertes was a cad.
> That Hamlet's treatment of Rosencrantz and Guildenstern was justified.
> That *Hamlet* would make a better cinema-film than stage-play.
> That *Hamlet* should be performed in modern dress.
> That it is better to read *Hamlet* than to see it acted.

56. Write a note on Shakespeare's use of prose, blank verse, and rhyme in this play.

57. What did the old lady mean who complained that *Hamlet* was " all quotations " ? Make a list of a dozen of them.

58. In one of its literary competitions, in January 1929, the *Observer* asked for a set of headlines for a modern newspaper, announcing the death of Ophelia.

ON THINKING IT OVER

Write these headlines. If you can give more than one set, in the manner of different newspapers, so much the better. (Don't be too solemn about it.)

59. Read *The Rehearsal*, by Maurice Baring, a one-act comedy about a rehearsal of *Macbeth* at the Globe Theatre, and then write a somewhat similar play about *Hamlet*. *The Rehearsal* is in *Nine Modern Plays*, T.E.S., No. 103. Or write a sequel to *Hamlet* in the form of a one-act burlesque play, and then, not before, compare it with *The New Wing at Elsinore*. (See " Further Reading.")

SIMPLER EXERCISES

Act I

60. Scene i. was written for performance in daylight on a stage with very little scenery, or none at all, and with the audience close to the actors. Re-read the scene carefully, and show how Shakespeare uses the opening dialogue to make us realize the time and place and the atmosphere of tense expectancy.

61. Is Scene i. a good opening scene for the play ? Compare it, if you can, with the first scenes of *The Tempest* or *Macbeth* and *As You Like It* or *Henry V*.

62. What have you learned from the first two scenes about the position of affairs in Denmark ?

63. What is Hamlet's state of mind in Scene ii. ?

64. What conclusion does Hamlet jump to as soon as he has heard about the Ghost ? Did Horatio and the others come to the same conclusion in Scene i. ?

65. Probably Shakespeare put the scene with Laertes, Ophelia, and Polonius in this position in the play in order to increase suspense. In what way does it do this ? Does it serve any other purpose ?

66. What are your first impressions of Polonius and Ophelia ?

67. While he is waiting for the Ghost to appear, Hamlet becomes eagerly interested in the talk about Danish drunkenness. What does this tell you about him ?

68. Write a paragraph about the Ghost's speech. Would it be more (or less) impressive if he described the " secrets of his prison-house " instead of only suggesting their horror ?

69. What do you think of Hamlet's behaviour in Scenes iv. and v. ? Is he mad ?

70. Imagine that you are Horatio, and describe briefly the events of Act I. so far as you are acquainted with them.

Act II.

71. After reading Scenes i. and ii., state briefly your opinion of Polonius, and Hamlet's opinion.

72. How does Hamlet treat Rosencrantz and Guildenstern in Scene ii. ?

73. Write a paragraph about the First Player's speeches, not forgetting to comment on the style.

74. Compare Hamlet's behaviour to Ophelia, as she describes it on pages 44–45, with his exhibition of " madness " to Polonius in Scene ii. There is a great contrast : what conclusions can you draw ?

75. What prompts Hamlet's soliloquy at the end of Scene ii. ? What are the faults of which he accuses himself, and is he right ? What is his plan " to catch the conscience of the King " ?

76. If you have read the soliloquy with care you will have noticed that it works up to a climax of self-disgust, and then falls away to a quieter tone. Where does the climax occur ?

77. Hamlet has not yet taken his revenge, and his soliloquy shows that he despises himself for it. What are the *real* reasons for his failure ?

ACT III.

78. What can be said for and against Ophelia's behaviour in Scene i.? Why does Hamlet treat her so brutally? Are you sorry for her?

79. What was Hamlet like before his father's death, according to Ophelia? Does he seem from this the kind of man who would find it easy to kill his uncle in cold blood?

80. Imagine that you are Rosencrantz, and describe the play-scene. You must make up your mind how much he knows at the beginning of the scene, and how much he guesses at the end.

81. What difference is there between the *style* of the " play within the play " and the play itself? Why has Shakespeare made this difference?

82. Do you think that the King's guilt is now known to the court at large?

83. Having read the play as far as Act III., Scene iii., say what you think of the King. Is he a great criminal, like Macbeth?

84. Hamlet's third great soliloquy (Scene i.) closely resembles a previous soliloquy of his : which is it?

85. Compare Hamlet's short soliloquy at the end of Scene ii. with his behaviour in Scene iii. Does he give his *real* reasons for not killing the King?

86. Does Hamlet kill Polonius in mistake for the King? If so, why does he stab him so promptly now after refraining in Scene ii.?

87. Do you think that Hamlet and the Queen still love one another?

88. Hamlet's position with regard to the King is very different now from what it was at the beginning of the act. Why?

Act IV.

89. What change have you noticed in Hamlet's treatment of Rosencrantz and Guildenstern, and their attitude to him ?   How do you explain it ?

90. Is the King really afraid of being blamed for the death of Polonius ?

91. Write a paragraph contrasting Hamlet and Fortinbras.

92. Hamlet's fourth great soliloquy, in Scene iv., is the clearest statement of his position that we have had.   Write a short summary of it, in the third person, and say which of the earlier soliloquies it most closely resembles.

93. Show how skilfully the King deals with Laertes.

94. What drove Ophelia mad ?   Do you think she committed suicide ?

95. After reading Scene vii., what do you think of Laertes ?

96. It has been suggested that Act IV. should really begin at what is now Scene iv.   (The divisions are not Shakespeare's.)   Would this be an improvement ?

97. Some of Shakespeare's plays lose interest in Act IV.   Is this true of *Hamlet* ?

Act V.

98. Criticize Hamlet's behaviour in the church-yard.

99. Tell the story of Hamlet's voyage and return, using all the details given in the play and no more.

100. Read again Hamlet's speech beginning : " Why, man, they did make love . . ." (Act V., Scene ii., page 133).   What do you learn from this about the *tone* in which Horatio made his remark

about Guildenstern and Rosencrantz. Have you noticed any other lines in which the speaker's tone is implied ?

101. If the part of the First Grave-digger had to be " doubled " with another character in a performance of the play, which should be the other character, and why ?

102. Say what you think of the humour in Scene i. Is it a welcome relief or not, and why should it come just here ?

103. What is wrong with Hamlet's apology to Laertes in the last scene ?

104. Does the play gain anything from the interview between Hamlet and Osric ?

105. Describe what happens in the last scene.

106. What does Horatio mean when he says " I am more an antique Roman than a Dane " ? Does this remind you of anything in *Julius Cæsar* and *Macbeth* ?

107. At the end of a tragedy Shakespeare usually leaves us with the feeling that life will now return to its ordinary course, and that there are competent, commonplace people left to deal with affairs. Is this true of *Hamlet* ?

GENERAL

108. If you read a short summary of *Hamlet* without having read the play, you would probably decide that it was melodrama (" a thriller ") and nothing else. The element of melodrama is certainly there, as in many tragedies which are successful stage-plays, but you know now that there is a great deal besides. What is it in *Hamlet* which raises the play from melodrama to great tragedy ?

109. In a study-circle which had just finished reading *Hamlet*, one of the members said, " What I want to know is whether these people ever really

existed. Because if not, it seems to me that we are just wasting our time, talking about things that never happened.''

What answer would you make?

110. If you had to abridge *Hamlet* for an amateur performance, how would you proceed, and what would be the chief '' cuts ''?—From a third to a half of the play would probably have to be omitted. When played at full length it takes five or six hours.

111. If you were acting in a performance of *Hamlet*, which part would you like to take, and why?

112. Make a list of six short passages in the play which are often quoted. If any of them are commonly misused, point this out.

113. Make a list of twelve words in the play which are now obsolete, and twelve which have changed in meaning, giving the Shakespearean meaning in each case.

114. If you had to choose from this play two brief extracts, one in verse and one in prose, to represent Shakespeare in an anthology of great passages from literature, which would you choose? Copy them out carefully and make a brief comment on each.

115. Invent a good title for each act of the play.

116. How old is Hamlet? Is the evidence in the play at all contradictory? Do you think that Shakespeare had made up his mind on this point?

117. Compare Hamlet with Brutus or Richard II. or Laertes.

118. Write a short defence of Ophelia.

119. Give three adjectives to describe the character of each of the following: Hamlet, Horatio, Claudius, Ophelia, Laertes, Polonius, Osric.

120. How does Laertes' position in Act IV. resemble Hamlet's position in Act I.? What difference have you noticed in the actions of the two avengers?

121. Sketch the character of any one in the play in whom you are interested.

ON THINKING IT OVER

122. What is Hamlet's opinion of Horatio? Is it correct?

123. Arrange one or more of the debates suggested in Section 55 above.

124. When he first hears from the Ghost the story of the murder, Hamlet declares that he will sweep to his revenge with wings as swift as meditation or the thoughts of love. Yet he delays for months, curses himself for doing so, declares that he has " cause and will and strength and means to do't," and stabs the King only when he himself is dying. His delay costs the lives of several people, and his own. How do you explain his failure to carry out his original intention?

FURTHER READING

(This list is made fairly comprehensive in the hope that some of the books may be available.)

For Comparison :

Shakespeare : *The Tragicall Historie of Hamlet Prince of Denmarke.* (An exact reprint of the First Quarto, 1603.) Edited by G. B. Harrison, with a good Introduction. (Bodley Head Quartos, John Lane, 3s.)

Shakespeare : *Richard II., Julius Cæsar, Macbeth,* " Teaching of English " Series.

For Criticism :

A. C. Bradley : *Shakespearean Tragedy.** (Macmillan, 12s. 6d.) A masterpiece of criticism which includes a very full study of *Hamlet.*

J. Dover Wilson : *What Happens in Hamlet.** (Cambridge Press, 12s. 6d.) A fresh and detailed study of the whole play, illuminating and exciting, which is worthy to rank with Bradley's.

* If only two books on *Hamlet* can be bought for the school library, these two are recommended.

HAMLET

A. T. Quiller-Couch : *Shakespeare's Workmanship.* (Benn, 9s.) A delightful book. Two chapters on *Hamlet.*

H. Granville-Barker : *From " Henry V." to " Hamlet."* (Oxford Press, paper covers, 1s.) An illuminating study of Shakespeare's development as a dramatist.

John Masefield : *Shakespeare.* (Home University Library, 2s. 6d.) An inspiring essay by a poet.

W. J. Lawrence : *Shakespeare's Workshop.* (Blackwell, 1928, 5s.) This includes essays on "Shakespeare's Workshop," " The Date of *Hamlet*," " The Mystery of the *Hamlet* First Quarto," and " The Ghost in *Hamlet.*"

For " Comic Relief " :

The New Wing at Elsinore, by St. John Hankin. (In *Ten Modern Plays*, Nelson. A burlesque sequel to *Hamlet* in one act : very easy to stage.

Rosencrantz and Guildenstern, by W. S. Gilbert. A burlesque of *Hamlet.*

The Golden Scilens, by J. C. Squire. (In *Grub Street Nights' Entertainments*.) A short story about a man who discovers the manuscript of *Hamlet* and makes a fortune.

For the Literary Background :

Allardyce Nicoll : *British Drama.* (Harrap, 12s. 6d. Illustrated.) The best history of our drama from the beginnings to the present day.

Ashley H. Thorndike : *Tragedy.* (Macmillan.) This historical study of English tragedy includes a section on the Elizabethan " revenge plays."

For a Survey of Modern Scholarship :

C. H. Herford : *A Sketch of Recent Shakesperean Investigation,* 1893–1923. (Blackie, 6s.) A brief and admirable essay which deals with biography, staging, publication of the plays, and critical interpretation.

For Stage Conditions :

Lamborn and Harrison : *Shakespeare, the Man and his Stage.* (World's Manuals, Oxford Press, 2s. 6d. Illustrated.)

W. J. Lawrence : *The Physical Conditions of the Elizabethan Public Playhouse.* (Oxford Press, 7s. 6d.)

For the Language :

George Gordon : *Shakespeare's English,* S.P.E. Tract No. XXIX. (Oxford Press, 1928. Paper covers, 2s. 6d.) This deals chiefly with vocabulary.

For Reference :

C. T. Onions : *A Shakespeare Glossary.* (Oxford Press, second edition, 1925, 5s.) This is based on the great *Oxford English Dictionary.*

A NOTE FOR AMATEUR DRAMATIC SOCIETIES

" *Let's Do a Play !* " by Rodney Bennett. Illustrated by Hugh Chesterman. (Nelson.) A complete guide to the production of plays, concerts, revues, musical plays, and all kinds of amateur performances, from the impromptu to the elaborate. It is thoroughly practical and written especially for small societies with scanty funds and equipment. The last 140 pages contain a very varied selection of plays, sketches, and recitations.

Producing School Plays, by Ernest F. Dyer, B.A., M.Ed. (Nelson.) This book deals with every phase of the production and staging of plays and musical plays in schools, and includes chapters on the work of the producer, rehearsals, settings, scene design, lighting equipment and its use, the performance, costume, the business side, the model stage, and the classroom and the stage, etc. There are twenty-two photographs of settings, etc., and fifty-two drawings. Written throughout from first-hand experience to meet the distinctive needs and problems of school dramatic work, its clear-sighted enthusiasm makes it also a valuable contribution to one of the most vital developments in English education to-day.

Shakespeare for Community Players, by Roy Mitchell. (Dent.) An invaluable book, with many excellent illustrations.

The Small Stage and its Equipment, by R. Angus Wilson. (Allen and Unwin.) Invaluable to the amateur, because it offers practicable solutions of the many problems of staging plays in small halls. Full instructions are given for constructing stages, making scenery, lighting equipment, etc. Many diagrams.

The Amateur Actor, by Frances Mackenzie. Illustrated. (Nelson.) This book shows the producer how to train amateur actors, and actors how to teach themselves. A fascinating series of exercises is included.

Stage Lighting, by C. Harold Ridge. (Heffer.) A treatise on the art and technique of the subject, which every dramatic society should possess.

A Book of Make-up, by Eric Ward. (Samuel French.) A practical handbook, with working illustrations.

British Costume during Nineteen Centuries, by Mrs. Charles A. Ashdown. (T. C. and E. C. Jack.) The best single-volume history : from the time of the Britons to 1820, with a special section on ecclesiastical dress. 578 illustrations in colour and line.

A List of Plays for Girls and Women, compiled by the British Drama League. (Nelson.) Over 200 plays are given in this list, carefully classified, with full details of each, and complete index.

A List of Plays for Boys and Men, compiled by the British Drama League. (Nelson.) Over 170 plays, arranged on the same lines as the above.

APPENDIX

Extracts from the First Quarto: *The Tragicall
Historie of Hamlet Prince of Denmarke.* 1603.

These passages are taken from Mr. G. B. Harrison's
excellent reprint : see " Further Reading."

Extract 1.   See page 67.

Corambis (*Cor.*) is Polonius.

King. See where hee comes poring vppon a booke.
> *Enter Hamlet.*
Cor. Madame, will it please your grace
To leaue vs here ?
Que. With all my hart.   *exit.*
Cor. And here *Ofelia*, reade you on this booke,
And walke aloofe, the King shal be vnseene.
Ham. To be, or not to be, I there's the point,
To Die, to sleepe, is that all ? I all :
No, to sleepe, to dreame, I mary there it goes,
For in that dreame of death, when wee awake,
And borne before an euerlasting Iudge,
From whence no passenger euer return'd,
The vndiscouered country, at whose sight
The happy smile, and the accursed damn'd.
But for this, the ioyfull hope of this,
Whol'd beare the scornes and flattery of the world,
Scorned by the right rich, the rich curssed of the poore ?
The widow being oppressed, the orphan wrong'd,
The taste of hunger, or a tirants raigne,
And thousand more calamities besides,
To grunt and sweate vnder this weary life,
When that he may his full *Quietus* make,

With a bare bodkin, who would this indure,
But for a hope of something after death ?
Which pusles the braine, and doth confound the sence,
Which makes vs rather beare those euilles we haue,
Than flie to others that we know not of.
I that, O this conscience makes cowardes of vs all,
Lady in thy orizons, be all my sinnes remembred.

Ofel. My Lord, I haue sought opportunitie, which
now I haue, to redeliuer to your worthy handes, a small
remembrance, such tokens which I haue receiued of you.

Ham. Are you faire ?

Ofel. My Lord.

Ham. Are you honest ?

Ofel. What meanes my lord ?

Ham. That if you be faire and honest,
Your beauty should admit no discourse to your honesty.

Extract 2.   See page 56.

Ham. Why I want preferment.

Ross. I thinke not so my lord.

Ham. Yes faith, this great world you see contents me
not,
No nor the spangled heauens, nor earth nor sea,
No nor Man that is so glorious a creature,
Contents not me, no nor woman too, though you laugh.

Extract 3.   See pages 73-74.

players My Lorde, wee haue indifferently reformed
that among vs.

Ham. The better, the better, mend it all together :
There be fellowes that I haue seene play,
And heard others commend them, and that highly too,
That hauing neither the gate of Christian, Pagan,
Nor Turke, haue so strutted and bellowed,
That you would a thought, some of Nature's journeymen
Had made men, and not made them well,
They imitated humanitie, so abhominable :
Take heede, auoyde it.

players I warrant you my Lord.

Ham. And doe you heare ? let not your Clowne speake
More then is set downe, there be of them I can tell you

That will laugh themselues, to set on some
Quantitie of barren spectators to laugh with them,
Albeit there is some necessary point in the Play
Then to be obserued : O t'is vile, and shewes
A pittifull ambition in the foole that vseth it.
And then you haue some agen, that keepes one sute
Of ieasts, as a man is knowne by one sute of
Apparell, and Gentlemen quotes his ieasts downe
In their tables, before they come to the play, as thus :
Cannot you stay till I eate my porrige ? and, you owe me
A quarters wages : and, my coate wants a cullison :
And, your beere is sowre : and, blabbering with his lips,
And thus keeping in his cinkapase of ieasts,
When, God knows, the warme Clowne cannot make a
    iest
Vnlesse by chance, as the blinde man catcheth a hare :
Maisters tell him of it.

    players We will my Lord.
    Ham. Well, goe make you ready.   *exeunt players*.

Extract 4. See pages 112 and 132.

Enter Horatio and the Queene.
  Hor. Madame, your sonne is safe arriv'de in *Den-marke*,
This letter I euen now receiv'd of him,
Where as he writes how he escap't the danger,
And subtle treason that the king had plotted,
Being crossed by the contention of the windes,
He found the Packet sent to the king of *England*,
Wherein he saw himselfe betray'd to death,
As at his next conuersion with your grace,
He will relate the circumstance at full.
  Queene Then I perceiue there's treason in his lookes
That seem'd to sugar o're his villanie :
But I will soothe and please him for a time,
For murderous mindes are alwayes jealous,
But know not you *Horatio* where he is ?
  Hor. Yes Madame, and he hath appoynted me
To meete him on the east side of the Cittie
To morrow morning.

     Cullison, a badge (*e.g.* master's coat of arms).
     Cinkapase (cinquepace), a dance with five steps.

Queene O faile not, good Horatio, and withall, com-
mend me
A mothers care to him, bid him a while
Be wary of his presence, lest that he
Faile in that he goes about.

Hor. Madam, neuer make doubt of that :
I thinke by this the news be come to court :
He is arriv'de, obserue the king, and you shall
Quickely finde, Hamlet being here,
Things fell not to his minde.

Queene But what became of *Gilderstone* and *Rossen-*
craft ?

Hor. He being set ashore, they went for *England,*
And in the Packet there writ down that doome
To be perform'd on them poynted for him :
And by great chance he had his fathers Seale,
So all was done without discouerie.

Queene Thankes be to heauen for blessing of the prince,
Horatio once againe I take my leaue,
With thowsand mothers blessings to my sonne.

Horat. Madam adue.

THE END